How to Pick a Winner

04

THE GINGER SERIES

how to pick a winner

mary mountier

AWA PRESS

First edition published in 2004 by
Awa Press, 149 Willis Street,
Wellington, New Zealand

ISBN 0-9582538-0-3

National Library of New Zealand Cataloguing-in-Publication Data
Mountier, Mary.
How to pick a winner / by Mary Mountier. 1st ed.
(The ginger series)
ISBN 0-9582538-0-3
1. Horse racing—Betting. 2. Gambling systems. I. Title. II. Series:
The ginger series (Wellington, N.Z.)
798.401—dc 22

Designed by Sarah Maxey
Cover illustration by Scott Kennedy
Typeset by Jill Livestre, Archetype
Printed by Astra Print, Wellington

This book is typeset in Walbaum

www.awapress.com

ABOUT THE AUTHOR

Mary Mountier has had a lifelong involvement with racing. As well as writing and editing six books on the subject, she has contributed essays on horsemen and women to the *Dictionary of New Zealand Biography*, written for New Zealand and overseas racing publications, and was the sole female voice on the Radio Racing Show throughout the 1980s. She served for six years on New Zealand's TAB board and in 1993 was awarded the New Zealand Suffrage Medal for services to racing. She lives on the Kapiti Coast with her husband Garry Ward.

CONTENTS

Why this book is a lie

LET'S GET SOMETHING clear from the start: the title of this book is a dreadful lie. If I really knew how to pick a winner, I wouldn't be writing about it. I'd be betting away in secret, squirrelling away millions, and not telling anyone how I was doing it. Because broadly speaking, with betting on horses (or dogs), the more people winning, the less the return.

That's something else I need to make clear. This book is not about picking a winner in rugby or prize petunias or life or politics. It's about picking winners on the racetrack. The fact this needs to be explained shows how far from the nation's psyche racing has fallen in recent times. I've seen headlines using the word 'racing' that are referring to *motor* racing! Just as nobody feels the need to include the word 'England' on that country's stamps, coins and various sporting bodies, people here used to regard horse racing in the same light. I even remember when racing commentaries were broadcast nationwide on the 'YA' stations – today's National Radio.

But although racing now attracts large crowds only on major Cup days and holiday or picnic meetings, it doesn't mean a sizeable number of people are not still fascinated by it. And a large part of that fascination lies in picking winners.

You don't actually have to *place* a bet to get the thrill of satisfaction when your choice comes first. All you need is someone to tell that you picked it. In fact, you don't even need to pick the *winner* to achieve some sort of satisfaction. Picking a horse that nearly won – or one that came in but, through an unfortunate set of circumstances, you didn't get your bet on – are also satisfactory stories to tell fellow racing fans. I remember when my brother was meant to put a £5 bet on for me at Trentham. Imagine my excitement when the horse duly won and paid over £20. My total collect, one hundred pounds, was a small fortune back then, especially to a 14-year-old. But Ted remembered about the bet only when the horse crossed the line, and refused to pay out, leading to years of debate about the ethical code of betting on behalf of others.

One of the reasons gambling on racing is so much more interesting than other forms of betting is because it contains those essential ingredients of skill and a certain control over the odds (even if only imagined) which are so sadly lacking in Lotto and gaming machines. These forms of gambling do not lead to heated discussions or newspaper columns. Imagine someone writing a regular column on the 'pokies'! The contrast between the intricacies and the rich history of racing and the banality of a slot machine could hardly be greater.

Racing is all about characters – both human and animal – good and bad, beautiful and ugly, sweet-natured and ill-tempered, champions and no-hopers. Getting to know these characters, even if only from a distance, is at the heart of racing. You don't bet on numbers, but on living creatures. And by their nature racing animals are capricious. Just when you think you've understood them, and can predict how they're going to run, they let you down. Trainers and owners need the patience of saints. So, to a lesser extent, do punters. If you're going to stay in the game, you have to learn several virtues, headed by optimism, tenacity and forgiveness.

The scope for discussing racing is endless. It is a known fact that conversations among racing followers are at once the most interesting and most boring in the world. Usually they are about how well or badly one's luck is going, and in return for telling your side (the interesting part) you have to listen to the other person's side (the boring bit).

Notice I mentioned 'luck'. Theoretically, the more you know about something, the better you get at it. So racing experts should consistently pick more winners than complete amateurs do. Over time, they probably do. But this is not the same thing as winning money through betting. That's where luck comes in — especially beginner's luck. Everyone who's taken a newcomer to the races has experienced it. There are countless reasons a certain horse has no hope of winning a certain race. The beginner backs it anyway. Because they like the name. Or number. Or the way the horse looks at them. The expert's pick runs down the track; the hopeless case wins.

That's called luck. It's also the glorious uncertainty of racing. And that's what you're up against when you try to pick a winner.

How it all
began for me

WHEN I WAS 12, my mother and two of my brothers took me to the Trentham races for the first time. I was instantly hooked. I loved the excitement, the atmosphere, the sights and sounds of the racecourse. I especially loved the thrill of choosing a horse (by its name, Baraden – no idea now why that appealed), being given ten shillings to bet with, and the horse coming in. I collected nearly £5. Possibly if Baraden had run a dismal last I would not be writing this book. Thinking back, Michael and Ted would have been only 16 and 17, and the legal age for betting was 21. I suppose Mum must have put all our bets on. Dad never set foot on a racecourse. He heartily disapproved of gambling, and only once in his life had a bet. I talked him into it. The horse's name was Simca, and it lost. The reason I was able to persuade him to spend five shillings (going halves with me in the bet) was that he had just bought a new Simca motor car. Cars were the one thing he liked spending money on.

Anyway, once hooked, I studied the *Turf Digest* each week assiduously, and listened to the races on the radio. I recall Peter Kelly, the commentator, describing the horses lining up at the start, and sometimes having to fill several minutes of air time when a fractious runner wouldn't go into the stalls. Then there was that gradually rising intonation of his commentary, which reached a high-pitched crescendo at the end, followed by either huge elation or huge disappointment, depending on how your horse had fared.

At secondary school I always sat at the back of the class so I could tuck the *Turf Digest* into my textbook. I knew the names of all the good horses, wonderful names like Roodyvoo (my all-time favourite), Hot Drop, Lucrative, Hush Money, Savage, Foglia D'Oro, Commanding, Resemblance, Even Stevens, Cheyenne, Marie Brizard, Rio Rapido, Action Packed – names that can still bring a frisson of pleasure. These days horses have names like Whatsundermykilt and Likeabatoutofhell and Goodgollymissmolly (you can't have more than 18 letters, and a space counts as a letter, so thatswhythey-areallruntogetherlikethat). I don't dislike them – they're kind of catchy – but you have to feel sorry for the poor commentators.

None of my school friends were interested in racing, but I remember when I was 17 dragging my first boyfriend out to Trentham. He was obsessed with car racing and found horses totally tedious. Another boyfriend was deeply shocked to find pictures of racehorses – pull-outs from *Hoofbeats* magazine – pinned up on my bedroom wall. He pointedly gave me a framed Picasso print. At around this time the nice lady from the Plimmerton TAB rang my mother and warned her not to let me put bets on until I was 21, as the inspectors had seen me there.

A few years later I found friends who loved the whole scene as much as I did. I even met up with some superior people who had tickets to the members' stand. In those days there was a long waiting list to become a member of the Wellington Racing Club, and the privilege was jealously guarded. No trainers or (horrors) jockeys were allowed into the stand proper. Only the elite entered. Everyone was formally dressed, and white-coated chaps turned away those who failed to meet the standard. The entire first level of the members' stand was barred to women. Children under 12 were barred everywhere. At one end of the first floor was the committee room. Many years later I became (I was told) the first woman to set foot in it, at the invitation of the president. The roof didn't fall in, but I got many glares of displeasure from the stuffier old stewards and their cronies.

My first venture into ownership came when a friend rang me one day and asked if I'd like a share in the next Melbourne Cup winner. (He later had a career in real estate.) This was in 1974, and the rules of racing had just been changed to permit syndicates of up to 25 people, making horse owning more affordable. Thus I became a member of New Zealand's first big syndicate. The horse, Clockstopper, didn't win the Melbourne Cup. In fact she raced only once, in a maiden event at Foxton, and finished last by 12 lengths.

Realising Clockstopper's future looked bleak, we acquired another horse, which we called Showstopper. Somebody pointed out that 'stopper' wasn't an ideal word to use in a racehorse's name, but we liked the continuity. Showstopper was a strikingly attractive black filly and it came as no surprise to us that she won four races as a two-year-old. We fully expected her to go on to be the star three-year-old of her season. When this didn't happen we sent her back to her breeder.

I've lost track of our succession of 'Stoppers', but by far the best turned out to be Heartstopper, who won the 1980 Manawatu Cup and three other races. She was much more satisfactory to watch than Showstopper because she was a stayer, so the races lasted longer.

Which reminds me: long races can confuse novice racegoers. Watching the Manawatu Cup with me were my husband Garry and his two children. Twelve-year-old Brendon and eight-year-old Ondine had never been to the races before. As Heartstopper went past the finishing post for the first time in the 2,300-metre race, she was last in the field of 17. Ondine let out a loud sigh and threw her two $1 tickets away. When, on the second time around, our bonny mare raced to the front (ridden to perfection by one of New Zealand's first and best women jockeys, Dianne Moseley), we scrabbled around frantically to find Ondine's tickets. And then, shamefully, Garry and I deserted the children and ran over to the members' stand to join in the Cup presentation and celebrations.

Heartstopper gave us our greatest thrill by being good enough to start in a Wellington Cup. Although she finished only seventh, it hardly mattered. We partied in the car park with a huge retinue of family and friends long before and long after the race.

Since then I've owned horses (and later dogs) on my own or in small partnerships, but the only one of note has been a greyhound named Stadium. A group of us formed a small syndicate to raise money for what is now referred to by everyone outside Wellington, but no one within, as the Cake Tin. Dear old Stadium did manage to win a few races, but I have to concede his earnings made little dent in the total needed.

King Charles II has a lot to answer for

NOW, A SPOT OF history to get things in perspective. Horses have been raced probably from the time they were first domesticated — at least 6,000 years ago, going by the cave drawings. It's a fundamental human instinct, once you've got past the business of staying alive, to say to your neighbour, 'I bet my plesihippus can run faster than yours.'

The ancient Egyptians, Greeks and Romans were big on chariot racing, the Arabs went in for endurance contests, and the Japanese raced Mongolian ponies when Britain was still inhabited by Picts and Celts. The first documented English racing goes back to 1540, when races were held at Chester, near Liverpool. (Note we're talking about *organised* racing – not the purely local or random races, usually for large wagers, that occurred before then. Records of these go back at least as far as King Edgar in the tenth century, and some historians claim the Roman invaders were into horse racing.)

Elizabeth I was the first English monarch to be seen 'at the races' – at Salisbury Plains in the 1580s. But the horses competing were not thoroughbreds, because that breed of horse, now the only breed used in galloping races, had not yet been created. (To be strictly accurate, some other breeds are used in galloping races – among them quarter-horses in the United States and pure Arabs in England – but these activities cannot be compared with the vast international sport of thoroughbred racing.)

But it is King Charles II, who came along nearly a century later, who's regarded, quite rightly, as the father of racing. You'll remember him – the one with long curly black hair, Nell Gwynn and other assorted mistresses, and a taste for living it up. Charles came to the throne after the downfall of Oliver Cromwell, that dreary old Puritan who turned Britain into a republic and disapproved of people having fun.

Charles's grandfather, James I, had built a royal palace at Newmarket, which he used as a base for hunting and hawking. James's son, Charles I, had introduced horse racing there, but these were rambling, 20-mile affairs.

The dashing new king turned Newmarket into a trendy modern racecourse.

Perhaps 'modern' is a slight exaggeration. Races were mostly run in four heats of four miles each, with half an hour's rest in between. Charles used to haul his entire court up from London twice a year so he could indulge in his favourite pastime, while keeping the country going on the side. He was a spectator, owner, breeder, rider, patron (today's 'sponsor') and adjudicator of the first proper rules, which he also helped formulate.

At first the horses were slow enough for the king and his court to keep up with as they galloped alongside: grandstands hadn't been invented then. Gradually the horses got faster, as Charles and his fellow enthusiasts spent fortunes importing lighter, sleeker, high-quality Arab and other Eastern stallions to mate with their existing mares. Thus the king unwittingly helped found a new breed of horse that eventually became known as the thoroughbred, and Newmarket became, and has remained, the headquarters of English racing.

And what began as a leisure activity of the nobility filtered down to the rest of English society. A love of horses, racing and gambling gave people across all classes and occupations an interest. And of course commerce rapidly developed around the sport, as horses were bred and trained, racecourses opened and betting blossomed. So Old Rowley, as Charles II was nicknamed (after his favourite riding horse) had not just indulged a passion:

he had fathered an industry that spread worldwide and is today worth billions of dollars.

How racing got started in New Zealand

NEW ZEALAND HAD no indigenous horses, let alone race-horses. The missionary Samuel Marsden brought three horses of mixed breed across from Australia in 1814, but they were for the purely practical purpose of transporting people and goods.

As the colony became more established, the settlers had time for a bit of recreation – and naturally their thoughts turned to horse racing. Most early horses were imported either directly from, or via, Australia. Figaro, who landed in Wellington in 1840, was the first authenticated thoroughbred stallion. He was bred in New South

Wales of impeccable English parentage, and made a lasting mark on racing stock through a mating with one of the few thoroughbred mares in New Zealand, who happened to be closely related: her sire, Emilius, was Figaro's grandsire.

From these tentative beginnings, the importation and breeding of thoroughbreds grew apace. With no other organised sport and little other public entertainment, the pioneers flocked to race meetings. As in England, the early racecourses were not enclosed, and therefore did not charge for admission. Funds came from leasing rights to refreshment and liquor booths, fees from bookmakers and gaming operators, and 'sweepstakes', often augmented by local businesses – the 'Publican's Purse' was usually the richest.

Most meetings consisted of a wide variety of activities, including foot races for men and children; races for ponies, donkeys, hacks and even bullocks; wrestling and boxing matches; cock fighting; side shows; games of chance; fortune tellers; refreshments, gaming booths, and musical entertainment in the form of a local band.

There is no precise documentation of New Zealand's first race meeting. Settlers in the Bay of Islands are said to have organised some races there in 1835, but if so the names of the winners were not written down. In Auckland in 1840, the newly arrived military garrison evidently ran some races, as Governor Hobson is noted as attending.

Wellington settlers staged the first recorded horse race – a hurdle event around Te Aro, with a couple of creeks to be crossed, for a prize of 15 guineas – as part of anniversary celebrations in January 1841. There were four entries, and the winner was Culmac Tartar, ridden by his owner Henry Petre. A year later what seems to have been the first full-scale race meeting, with a published programme, was held at 'Epsom Downs', Auckland.

In October 1842 Figaro became the first thoroughbred to race here, beating Culmac Tartar on the beach at Petone, at the north end of Wellington Harbour. This was part of a 'proper' raceday. A general holiday was declared and most of Wellington's population, both European and Maori, attended. A contemporary account stated, 'The Clerk of the Course had a busy day arranging with Te Puni [a local chief] to have the native dogs tied up and the pigs kept at home and imploring whalers to push their boats out far enough to give the horses a clear course … The day closed with a dinner for the gallants at Barrett's Hotel.'

This was exactly the sort of thing that displeased the curmudgeonly Scot Alexander Marjoribanks, who wrote in his 1846 book *Travels in New Zealand*, 'It is curious that the English cannot settle down quietly, even in a new country, without wasting their time and money on those most absurd of all absurdities – horse racing and public dinners.'

From Mr Marjoribanks' point of view, matters rapidly went from bad to worse. Racecourses were laid out in almost every area the English settled – and some which they did not, for Maori also took to horse racing with enthusiasm. Chiefs and tribes acquired their own horses, some as payment for land, and set up racecourses on tribal land. Young Maori men proved to be naturally skilled and fearless riders, and for many years most European race meetings included a 'Maori' race. With thoroughbreds still a rarity, these early meetings catered for stock and carriage horses, hacks and ponies, and often included a trotting race (in the saddle).

Like most of the early settlers' clubs and courses, the Maori race meetings have long since vanished, with the sole exception of the Otaki-Maori Racing Club, 75 kilometres north of Wellington, which is still going strong.

The proliferation of early racing clubs in the South Island, especially Otago and Southland, reflected the transient nature of New Zealand's population. At the height of the 1860 to 1880s' gold rush, dozens of clubs were formed. Most entries were utility hacks, ridden by their owners.

Some meetings were well organised, but many operated under rough and ready rules. An account of an early meeting at Naseby, in the heart of the goldfields, noted that lead must have been in short supply. To make up the required weight, one of the riders strapped half a sack of potatoes to his saddle. Riding vigorously, he brushed past the leader, and in so doing burst the bag and potatoes spilt out all over the course. The report notes, 'Apparently weighing-in was not so carefully checked as nowadays, as the judge's placings were not disturbed.'

Nelson became the first region to seriously race thoroughbreds, thanks to Henry Redwood (dubbed 'Father of the New Zealand turf') and other influential sportsmen who settled there. As early as 1845 they held a meeting at Stoke, and the Nelson Jockey Club was formed in 1848, the same year as Wanganui, the oldest racing club still surviving. Wanganui is also credited with being the first club in New Zealand to stage a full-scale trotting meeting, in 1881.

Canterbury was another hotbed of affluent racing enthusiasts, with races first held in Hagley Park in 1851. Within a few decades it was also a centre for light harness racing, along with Otago and Southland, where trotting races had been held as part of gallops meetings since 1864. In those days many horse enthusiasts competed in both types of racing, among them the famous thoroughbred trainer Dick Mason. Christchurch and Dunedin became the leading racing centres, offering the largest stake money and the most important events. It was not until 1913 that the Auckland Cup overtook the New Zealand Cup (run at Riccarton, Christchurch) in value.

By the close of the nineteenth century, Dick Mason was private trainer for Henry Redwood, and the partnership was cleaning up most of the big galloping races. The organisation and rules of racing were well established, with national controlling bodies for both galloping and trotting; paid handicappers and club secretaries had been introduced; and the totalisator (from which government duty was extracted) was helping fund it all. While a few clubs had initially been run for private profit, New Zealand's racing leaders had decided the sport should be set up on a non-proprietary basis, with all profits channelled back into it — a system still operating today (unlike overseas, where privately owned courses are common).

And New Zealand-bred horses had already won two Melbourne Cups — Martini-Henri in 1883 and Carbine in 1890. The New Zealand thoroughbred breeding industry, famed for producing durable stayers, was flourishing.

Since then racing in New Zealand has been through many cycles, surviving two world wars, the 1930s' Depression and the 1987 share crash. Its heyday was probably the 1950s and '60s, when horse numbers and racetrack attendance reached a peak, and off-course TAB betting grew exponentially. At the bottom of each cycle, pessimists invariably predict that racing will be lucky to survive — but then they said that about the movies.

What is a thoroughbred, anyway?

ATHOROUGHBRED HORSE is a genetically distinct breed, in the same way a Clydesdale, Shetland pony or Appaloosa is. But because it's such a nice word, 'thoroughbred' is often used as a synonym for 'high class' and 'pure bred', which is also its meaning in direct translation from the Arabic *Kehilan*.

You get a 'breed' of horse (or any other animal) by selecting individuals that exhibit the traits you're after, such as running fast, and mating them. Often this involves inbreeding (mating siblings, and even parents to offspring), which is the quickest way of standardising a breed. This is what initially happened with the thoroughbred. Once there are sufficient numbers with the desired characteristics, and they're consistently passing these characteristics on to their offspring, the group can be called a breed.

The most astonishing fact about thoroughbreds is that they all trace back in direct male line to just three stallions: the Godolphin Arabian, the Byerley Turk and the Darley Arabian. Even more astonishingly, more than 95 percent go back to just one of these, the Darley Arabian.

Many people find this hard to believe. But unlike humans, for whom – unless you're a member of royalty or similar – genealogy gets a bit blurry beyond a few generations, a thoroughbred's pedigree can be traced back to its roots. And that's not all. The breeding and performance of practically every one of a thoroughbred's ancestors are on record. How many of us can even name our great-great-grandparents, let alone describe what they did? Quite simply, the thoroughbred is the best documented of all animal species, and no other organised sport has a longer recorded history.

I should point out that although the direct male line is undoubtedly important, it's by no means the whole story. Nor is there anything especially magical about direct male – or female – lines. By the time you go back even ten generations, you have a total of 2,046 individual ancestors, who theoretically have all passed on at least some of their genes. At 20 generations the total is over two million, by which time the early gene pool has become pretty diluted.

Today's thoroughbreds are up to about 40 generations down the line. However, by concentrating on certain strains, breeders have emphasised good traits and (they hope) eliminated bad. Thus the best of the breed occur much more frequently in pedigrees. Researchers at Dublin's Trinity College in the 1970s discovered that, in terms of overall genetic contribution to the current thoroughbred population, the Godolphin Arabian was, surprisingly, way ahead of the Darley Arabian, and an obscure horse called the Curwen Bay Barb relegated the Byerley Turk to fourth.

If you're wondering about these names, I don't blame you. The thing is, three centuries ago horses were usually named after their owners. Mr Darley, Captain Byerley, the Earl of Godolphin and Mr Curwen were merely the last owners of the above-mentioned stallions, all of which were imported from exotic parts of the world, loosely known as 'the Orient', between 1689 and 1730.

(This practice caused confusion when a horse was sold, because its name would change to the new owner's. Some horses with several different names are now considered to be one and the same horse.)

There are several romantic stories attached to the Godolphin Arabian. The first is that he was bought for a few pounds in Paris after he was spotted pulling a water cart. The second is that he was supposedly sent as a 'teaser' to Lord Godolphin's stud, and when the resident sire refused to mate with the mare, Roxana, the Arabian served her instead. That's the low-key version. The bodice-ripper one claims the two horses fought for the favours of the lovely Roxana and the Godolphin won. The other stallion was called Hobgoblin, which could hardly have helped.

Either way it's a load of old cobblers, and I put these stories in only for light relief. Even the water-cart one is now considered highly improbable. Much more likely is that the Godolphin Arabian originated from one of the royal studs of Morocco or Algiers, and was given to the King of France by the Bey of Tunis. This is an important point, because at some later date he began to be referred to as the Godolphin *Barb*.

According to Lady Wentworth, whose family was famous for its breeding of Arabian horses, and who wrote the definitive book on the origins of the thoroughbred, no Eastern royal stud would have harboured a Barb, as it was considered greatly inferior to the Arab horse. As she put it, 'The Arabian is the Tap Root, the Barb a derivation which could no more stamp itself on a whole breed of racehorses than any other cross-bred pony.'

What's more, you could buy a Barb at that time for a mere 20 guineas, whereas the going price for a good Arabian was between £1,000 and £3,000. The Duke of Newcastle, a horseflesh authority of the day, was quoted as saying, 'The Barb is so lazy and negligent in his walk as he will stumble on a bowling green, and he trots like a cow...' (Take note, owners, for future insults of rival horses.)

As for the 'Turks' – as in the Byerley Turk – well they didn't exist at all! Those careless old horse buyers in the seventeenth century called horses Turks if they happened to acquire them in Turkey. They were almost certainly Arabs.

Legend has it that all pure-bred Arab horses trace back to the five mares of Mohammed. While evolutionary research shows they probably developed from a primitive wild horse living in the highlands of Arabia, the strict commandments laid down in the Koran undoubtedly helped maintain the breed's purity and quality. Even today, enthusiasts often develop a fanatical attitude to Arab horses, rating them way above all other breeds for their vitality, spirit and almost ethereal beauty. And it must be said that with their exquisite proportions, arched neck, 'dished' head, large luminous eyes, high tail carriage, and the long, graceful trotting action that makes them appear to 'float', they do give an impression of refinement and elegance.

Certain strains of thoroughbreds have retained their Arab qualities more than others. I remember seeing a sire called Standaan at a New Zealand stud some years ago. He was pure white (grey horses get progressively whiter as they age), and when he was brought out for inspection by our group there was an audible collective intake of breath, such was his beauty and quality.

Getting back to those original three stallions, they were not the only ones to establish thoroughbred male lines; many more Eastern horses contributed to the mix. However, by about 1850 all of their direct male lines had died out, and the Arab cross had ceased to further improve the thoroughbred breed.

All this talk about sires may lead you to think the mares didn't count. Of course they did. It's just that nobody is sure who or what the 'foundation mares' were. Lady Wentworth, true to her obsession with pure Arabs, maintains that all the foundation mares in the first English stud book were Eastern in origin, and the majority Arabs. That begs the question: if the mares were Arabs, and we know most of the stallions were, how come they didn't breed true to type – that is, more Arabs?

The assertion they were native English stock is equally unconvincing. The only horses native to England were various breeds of small ponies and big draught-horse types, although it is true that the indigenous galloway ponies were once used for racing, and over the centuries some were likely to have been crossed with Eastern breeds to make them speedier and bigger.

So the best summation of the foundation mares' identity is that they were 'of mixed pedigree'. And it is generally agreed that today's thoroughbreds trace back to only about a dozen mares, of which one of the most important was named Old Bald Peg, poor dear.

The physical evidence of the modern thoroughbred shows that, except for a few distinctive bloodlines, it has evolved away from the Arab. As a rule, it is taller, faster, more heavily muscled and 'coarser' in appearance. In the process of evolution it has also increased in height by about one and a half hands (15 centimetres), and correspondingly in physical strength, scope, length of stride and speed. Today's thoroughbreds are much faster than those of 100 years ago, although some of the improvement is simply the result of better tracks, equipment, training and riding methods, and better nutrition. Speed is of course by no means the only attribute breeders want in a racehorse: other essentials are courage, determination and soundness.

Breeding theories come and go. Enthusiasts are liable to become messianic in their promulgation of them, but modern genetics are helping us understand why most don't work – at least not consistently. If they did, Phar Lap's full brothers and sisters would also have been champions, which they weren't. You only have to look at your own siblings to see the point.

Much of the lasting fascination of racing is inextricably linked to the challenge of breeding better horses, the only true test of which is on the racetrack. Just as in King Charles's day, very rich people spend very large amounts pursuing this goal.

Hobby breeders pursue the same goal on modest budgets. Every time the 'battlers' succeed, it raises the hopes of thousands, and shifts racing news on to the front page. Kiwi and Bonecrusher did this in New Zealand, Bernborough and Vo Rogue in Australia, and Seabiscuit most famously of all in America.

Why trotting
is different

IF THE ENGLISH can claim to have invented thoroughbreds, Americans get the credit for standardbreds. This is the other main type of racehorse, and is used in what was once called 'trotting' but is now termed 'harness racing', covering the two gaits, trotting and pacing. Harness horses developed from a different type of animal. Which is not surprising, when you think about it. Imagine you're living in the days before cars and trucks. If you're being pulled along in a cart behind a horse, it is much more comfortable if the horse goes at a smooth, steady trot, rather than a canter or gallop. It's also safer. And it's better if the horse pulling your carriage has a quiet temperament, rather than high spirits and a tendency to bolt.

So here you have the fundamental difference: thoroughbreds are good at going flat out, don't usually have a comfortable trotting action, tend to be flighty and are easily spooked; standardbreds, by contrast, are naturally smooth trotters or pacers, and much more sensible and well-mannered. To most people they look the same, but after a while you'll notice that trotters and pacers tend to have shorter, thicker necks and bigger heads – although that doesn't make them any less beautiful, I hasten to add.

The origins of harness racing as an organised sport are rather hazy. It was not invented by Harry Nicoll, a pioneer in Canterbury trotting, as some locals assumed at the time. The classical Greek poet Homer mentions a trotting race in his epic *Iliad*, but the earliest 'modern' races were recorded in 1799 in Moscow – the place where the Orlov Trotter evolved from Count Alexis Orlov's experimental breeding of Arab stallions and Friesian mares. Better known in his day as one of Catherine the Great's lovers, Count Orlov turned from a successful career as admiral of the Russian fleet to an even more successful one as a horse breeder. For a long time, until it was overtaken by the American standardbred, the Orlov Trotter was the fastest in the world. It was also tough enough to stand around in freezing Russian winters when used as a carriage horse.

Meanwhile, in other parts of the world, trotters were being developed for racing from various breeds. The Norfolk Trotter came from east England, where trotting (or 'ambling' – the old term for pacing) was popular until galloping pushed it into the background. Oddly enough, it has never recovered. In Britain harness racing now exists only as a small-scale, hobby sport in north-east England, Wales and Scotland.

Trotting races were recorded in Padua, northern Italy, in the early 1800s, and around the same time on the east coast of North America. New York had a racetrack in Harlem, where in 1806 the amazing feat of a trotter named Yankey covering a mile in less than three minutes was written up with wonderment. A century later the standardbred mare Lou Dillon would do the same distance in two minutes.

The term 'standardbred' is based on the extremely practical idea of measuring how fast a horse can cover a mile in a trot. The standard set then was 2 minutes 30 seconds. Today it's 2 minutes 15 seconds for three-year-olds and up, but good horses regularly better 2 minutes. Pacers go a few seconds faster.

When the breed and sport were getting under way, a trotter had to be able to pass the standard test (now called 'qualifying time') to be allowed to race in public, or be included in the American Trotting Register. This possibly accounts for the greater preoccupation with times in harness racing than in galloping.

There is a proliferation of records set by different age groups, over different distances and under different conditions. Most modern records are from a moving start, and American tracks are designed to achieve the fastest times. Hence America holds all the current world records, including an astonishing 1 minute 50.2 seconds for a mile trot, set in 2004.

The improvement in times over the years is due not just to selective breeding and better training methods, but to better tracks and, most of all, lighter, better-designed sulkies with pneumatic tyres. The original racing sulkies were high, heavy, hickory-wheeled contraptions, with the driver sitting up almost level with the horse's back. Some even had four wheels.

Many of the early races and time trials, however, were with riders in the saddle. Saddle trotting and pacing were common well into the twentieth century, and are still popular in France. Believe it or not, New Zealand champion Cardigan Bay, the first standardbred in the world to win a million dollars, competed in a saddle pacing race at Omakau, Central Otago, early in his career. (He was beaten by a nose in a field of 19.)

But trotting as we know it today really got started in America around the mid-nineteenth century. By this time sulkies were in general use and that other gait, pacing, had begun to gain in popularity. Trotting, I should explain, is a diagonal gait, the same system a baby uses when it crawls. Pacing is where the legs on the same side move forward at the same time. It is smoother and slightly faster, although not suited to rough ground because the hooves skim along the surface. Although it's seen as an unnatural gait, some animals such as elephants and camels are natural pacers.

The American standardbred came from a blending of thoroughbreds, Norfolk Trotters, Hackneys, Cleveland Bays and Morgans. The Morgan name comes from Justin Morgan, who owned a half-thoroughbred stallion, born around 1789. To supplement the family income, Morgan (the horse) was used to impregnate neighbouring farmers' mares. He proved extremely prepotent, passing on such desirable qualities as stamina, speed, courage, good nature and good looks.

But by far the most influential individual horses in the development of standardbreds were the English thoroughbred Messenger and his great-grandson Hambletonian. The grey Messenger arrived in America in 1788, at a time when horse racing there was going through a slump. Consequently he stood at stud for a very modest fee, and served all kinds of mares, from cart horses to thoroughbreds.

When he died in 1808 he was buried with full military honours. The lengthy inscription on his grave-stone includes the words, 'No stallion ever imported in this country did more to improve our horse stock' and 'Among his descendants is every two-minute trotter'. This suggests the inscription was installed many years after his death, because it wasn't until Hambletonian's stud career half a century later that Messenger's profound influence on trotting horses became apparent. Today both horses have races named after them, including the prestigious Messenger Stakes in New Zealand.

The importation of standardbreds into New Zealand in significant numbers around the early 1880s marked the beginning of trotting as a fully fledged, organised sport. Before that, trotting races had been held as part of galloping programmes, or as private contests. The horses and ponies used had been a mixture of breeds, with their main occupation being pulling carts and carriages. It was only when the sporting pioneers began spending serious money on American standardbreds that trotting horses were kept solely for racing.

Greyhounds are the true aristocrats

THE MODERN sport of greyhound racing goes back only to the twentieth century, but the breed itself is thousands of years old. Ironically, although greyhound racing is these days seen as the poor relation of horse racing, it uses dogs that were once the symbol of aristocracy. The Pharaohs kept an early version as pets. Ancient Grecian art and coins depict short-haired hounds virtually identical to modern greyhounds. And in medieval Britain, killing a greyhound was punishable by death. The dogs were greatly prized for the same reasons they are today: their intelligence, agility, strong hunting instinct, and extreme speed.

Greyhounds hunt by sight, not smell, and can spot a moving object up to a kilometre away. The ancient practice of coursing – chasing a live hare – was a favourite pastime of the early Romans, who brought both dogs and European hares with them when they conquered Britain. It also appealed to the English nobility, who from the Middle Ages were the only ones allowed to keep and hunt with greyhounds. Queen Elizabeth I (clearly something of a sporting buff) was responsible for having rules for competitive coursing drawn up. These were still in effect when the first official club was founded 200 years later at Swaffham, Norfolk, by the notorious Lord Orford (see page 101).

Unlike modern greyhound racing, where six or eight dogs compete, coursing involved only two dogs being released at a time, with points allotted for speed and skill, as well as for the kill (worth only one point). As the Roman historian Arrian wrote in 124 AD, the purpose was not to catch the hare, but to enjoy the chase. Romans were even more sporting-minded than the English, letting only one dog at a time chase the hare, which had to be given a fair start and often escaped.

In mid-eighteenth century England, greyhound enthusiasts began to keep proper pedigrees of their dogs, and the Earl of Orford began his famous breeding experiments. Over the following century the popularity of coursing increased enormously and the Waterloo Cup meet, first held near Liverpool in 1837, became the premier competition. It was a major national event, in its heyday attracting daily crowds of 70,000 and huge publicity. Most countries have long since banned coursing, but the Waterloo Cup is still contested and England's National Coursing Club has 23 affiliates. Like foxhunting, however, it faces an uncertain future.

By the mid-1880s, the evolution towards enclosed tracks had started. Instead of vast open-country courses, large fenced parks, with escape holes for the hares, were formed. But even in the nineteenth century some people thought chasing live prey was cruel, and experiments using artificial lures were tried. The first was at Hendon, England, in 1876, when a motorised stuffed rabbit was set up on a long straight rail and chased by six dogs. For various reasons, not the least being the tedium of the straight track, it failed to catch on.

Thirty years later an American called Owen Patrick Smith began work on a similar idea. Smith's first public experiment, at Salt Lake City in 1907, used a motorbike to pull the lure, but he later patented an 'inanimate hare conveyor' and eventually, in California in 1919, the modern form of greyhound racing was born. The key was the oval track, which brought the athletic skills and tracking instincts of the dogs to the fore. This was quickly adopted elsewhere and gradually perfected, although even today mechanised lures occasionally fail.

In New Zealand, coursing developed when hares imported by English settlers became pests, and greyhounds were brought in to combat them. Coursing clubs sprang up, mainly in Auckland and the bottom half of the South Island. New Zealand even had its own Waterloo Cup, which in 1919 combined with Australia to become the Australasian Waterloo Cup.

By the time New Zealand officially abolished coursing in 1954, 'drag hare' track racing, using a rabbit skin attached to a line, and other more sophisticated artificial lures, had overtaken it as the preferred sport involving dogs. In 1934 Auckland's Western Springs hosted the first public exhibition of the drag lure. An account in *The New Zealand Herald* described how, at the end of the race, the 'hare' would be pulled under a sack screen 'round which the dogs would gather in a puzzled manner. They were even more bewildered when the leaders proved too fast for the quarry and seized it ... the excited and suspicious actions of the dogs as they cautiously examined the strange object created great amusement among the crowd.'

Clubs in other centres followed suit, experimenting with different kinds of tracks and lures. But greyhound enthusiasts had a mighty battle when they wanted to move from amateur to professional status. Use of the totalisator was the key to advancement, but galloping and trotting authorities did all they could to prevent, or at least postpone, this happening. It was not until 1981 that full off-course as well as on-course totalisator facilities were permitted for greyhound meetings in New Zealand.

In England greyhound racing is the third most popular spectator sport (after soccer and rugby league), but in New Zealand it remains in the shadow of horse racing. However with dog numbers expanding to meet demand, and its niche slot on the TAB Trackside television channel helping attract an annual off-course turnover of around $85 million, greyhound racing is now unquestionably part of the scene.

Yet the dogs themselves have an image problem. Because greyhounds have to wear muzzles on the racetrack, outsiders think they must be vicious. In fact they are gentle, normally good-natured and laid-back dogs who, given half a chance, become lounge lizards in retirement and make excellent pets.

Social status
in racing

RACING IS FRIGHTFULLY snobbish. Don't believe people who try to tell you otherwise.

At the top of the tree are the thoroughbreds. First, they've been around longer, and second, they were created by England's ruling classes as a sporting horse, to run faster than other horses in races, and were temperamentally not much suited to anything else. Certainly nothing as useful as pulling carriages. Therefore only the rich could afford to indulge in owning and breeding thoroughbreds.

By contrast, standardbred racing developed as a sideline to these horses' practical function of trotting or pacing smoothly over long distances, and being docile enough to put into harness. The early colonial settlers tended to look down their noses at trotting horses, describing them as ill-bred, which many of them were.

At the bottom of the scale is greyhound racing, because dogs are the cheapest of all to train and race. In this part of the world theirs is the newest of the three codes. Except for a few standout races, the prize-money is relatively low. To many people actively involved in galloping, greyhounds are simply beyond the pale, and trotters aren't much better. For them, there are 'real' racehorses, Ben Hurs and plate-lickers, in that order. Most serious punters prefer one or the other, although the truly dedicated gambler bets on all three. In New Zealand, betting turnover on gallops is roughly twice that on trotting, with the dogs a distant third.

Then within the codes themselves there are layers of prestige – again, usually related to the intrinsic value of the animal. In England, the perceived difference between 'flat' racing and steeplechasing is so great that each has its own controlling body – the National Hunt for jumping and the Jockey Club for flat racing.

Competing over jumps is, logically, much more demanding than running along on the flat. But apart from a handful of events like the notorious English Grand National and the completely dotty Maryland Hunt Cup (see page 94), jumping races have, on average, lower prize-money, attract far less reflected glory, and are regarded with disdain in some racing circles. One reason is that horses and dogs too slow or old to win on the flat are often tried 'over the sticks': few stables specialise in jumpers. Nevertheless, to most onlookers, hurdles and steeplechases are hugely exciting. I usually shut my eyes when a big fence is looming. Someone told me that an old jumps' jockey did the same thing, which was why he wasn't scared. Actually, I've always thought skydiving is for people who aren't brave enough to ride in steeplechases.

In harness racing, trotters are widely seen as the poor relations of pacers. (For an explanation of the difference, see page 32.) It used to be the other way round, but today much bigger stake money and many more events are offered for pacers – at least in this part of the world. (Pacing has never caught on in Europe.) This is despite the fact that trotters are more durable, have more stamina and usually keep racing to much older ages than pacers. And to the casual observer the trotting gait, with its greater variation, is more pleasing to watch than the more mechanical, regular pace. Aficionados of trotting may well ponder the perverseness of it all.

From the animals' point of view, athletic or breeding ability can have far-reaching consequences. In short, the better you perform, the better you're treated. True champions are often indulged like spoilt children. The Roman Emperor Caligula carried this to extremes by making his favourite racehorse, Incitatus, a senator, with all the attendant luxuries. The great New Zealand sire Sir Tristram expected and got fresh grass fed to him in his stall around midnight. The champion mare Sunline was notorious for bucking off her work rider and devoted 'strapper' Claire Bird who, brushing aside a broken nose, black eyes and smashed hand, only loved the mare all the more for her fiery spirit.

At the other end of the scale, few owners will pay to keep an animal in training once it is apparent it's never going to win (although there are exceptions — see Haru-urara, page 107). While being trained, most horses and dogs are well cared for. This is a simple matter of economics. Animals that are fed nutritiously (often better than their trainers), properly exercised and have ailments attended to will perform better. And performance on the racetrack — either its own or its offsprings' — is the ultimate measure of an animal's value. When the value drops too low the pampering stops. Fortunately, in most western countries animal welfare laws protect these demoted horses and dogs from outright neglect. Many are used for alternative sports, or simply kept as pets. The rest, sadly, end up being euthanased.

Another area of snobbery relates to jockeys. This is a hangover from racing's origins in England, where jockeys were regarded as on a par with domestic servants, although with rather lower morals. Even the most successful riders seldom bridged the class gap. In 1886 the Earl of Suffolk called for the Jockey Club to take action over 'the unwholesome system of lavishing extraordinary rewards for very slight services. It is impossible that jockeys can be kept in their proper position when successful members of the riding fraternity are able to realise fortunes of £100,000 and more within a dozen years of their first appearance in the saddle.'

In New Zealand's more egalitarian society such attitudes were less common, but even today the idea lingers in some circles that jockeys are inferior to those who employ them. In reality, they deserve the highest admiration for their skill and courage – not to mention getting up at 4 a.m. each day and half-starving themselves. Riding a galloping racehorse at speeds of up to 60 kilometres an hour in a tightly packed field is one of the most dangerous occupations on earth. Top jockeys have always made a lot of money, but they do so by putting their lives on the line every time they go to work. And average jockeys take the same risks for very modest returns.

Professional trainers historically have come somewhere between owners and jockeys on the social scale, but again the distinction in New Zealand has always been less pronounced than in England, partly because there are so many owner-trainers. These days leading trainers are likely to be wealthier and better educated than many owners. It is not an easy life, however. For most it is not even a rewarding one, and many supplement their income by buying and selling horses to overseas stables.

Trainers have to select the optimum race programme for each horse, get the animals fit and peaking at the right time, hire jockeys or drivers, take responsibility for staff and stables, oversee documentation, organise horse transport (which may include air travel overseas), pay bills and deal with owners. In other words, live in a state of constant worry.

So you want to be an owner?

PEOPLE BECOME owners of racing animals for a variety of reasons. The most common are that you've been born into a racing family and simply carry on the tradition, or that you're talked into it in a weak moment by a friend. 'Ownership', by the way, is the word used even if you own only a tiny percentage of an animal, and even if it is only leased to you.

Whether you stay being an owner depends on your temperament and the animal's success. If you're a natural optimist you keep going, even if you never own a winner. Some people have stuck it out for 20 years before tasting success. If, however, you are an impatient or pessimistic person you won't stay in the game, even if you get a really good horse or dog at the beginning. That's because sooner or later your animal will lose, get injured or be put out for a spell, or the next one you get will not be as good.

Another reason for disillusionment is when someone has told you this is a good way to make money. Only really clever or really lucky people make money out of owning racing animals. (Breeding them is a different matter.) The lure of riches is the worst possible motivation for becoming an owner, believe me. But there are many other reasons for doing it. Having fun is the best one. The adrenaline rush of seeing your horse win is another. It's much safer than bungy jumping and some people rate it above sex.

Of the various kinds of ownership in which I've been involved, the most enjoyable is undoubtedly the large syndicate. You use it as an excuse to have regular parties, both on-course and off. It is therefore preferable to belong to a syndicate where most members live in the same region.

It is also good to have your horse trained locally. That way the really keen members can get up ridiculously early to watch it do track work. It is a completely meaningless exercise for most people, who can seldom recognise their own horse, let alone tell if it's going well. But you get to breathe in the authentic atmosphere of stables and tracks, and hear the authentic swearing and snorting that makes you feel you're really part of racing.

A tip: since few horses win a lot of races (actually most don't win any, but don't let that small fact put you off), it's advisable to make the most of every victory you're lucky enough to have. Unless you're a hardened old hack yourself, watching your horse win the humblest maiden race is every bit as euphoric as watching it win a Cup or Derby.

At the time, that is. The lead-up excitement of having a runner in a major race, plus the aftermath of counting up the stake money and basking in the glory greatly embellishes the experience. It will also provide the starting point for conversations with fellow racegoers or taxi drivers for years to come. And the more important the event, the more your social status will be enhanced. Owners of Melbourne Cup winners will be introduced as such for the rest of their lives. It is more prestigious, in some circles, than a knighthood. In fact, since New Zealand doesn't have knighthoods any more, it could be regarded as a suitable substitute.

If it's just winners you want, however, dogs are a better bet than horses, and much cheaper to run. Because of the way greyhound racing is structured, and because there is a maximum of eight dogs in a race, all but the slowest dogs will win eventually. On the other hand, there is nowhere near the kudos and hype attached to dog racing. In this part of the world, even the biggest meetings fail to attract the big hats, champagne parties and thousands of cheering onlookers that go with big-time horse racing.

The rule with syndicates is the bigger the better. As I've pointed out, you are most unlikely to make any money, so dividing winnings among a multitude of members is not a concern. Remember, too, that the more there are of you, the less your share of the animal's up-keep – and this is always more than expected on account of thoroughbreds, in particular, being the hypochondri-acs of the animal world. If your horse earns enough to pay for its oats, consider yourself fortunate. If it also pays the veterinary bills, you are extraordinarily lucky.

There is one immutable rule of ownership: always back your own animal, even when the trainer has told you it has no show and is in the race only for the exercise or experience. You can back all the others too, if you like, but there is a binding law that you must show faith in your animal by having a bet on it, however small.

The evils of
gambling ...

RIGHT, LET'S LOOK into
betting. Why do we gamble? It's
a basic human instinct – the
thrill of the unpredictable and
the huge satisfaction gained from 'beating the odds'.
Certain cultures seem more predisposed toward gambling than others. Asian and Australian come to mind,
with New Zealand fast catching up. And therein lies a
problem. If enough people think too many of their fellow
citizens are gambling too much, they make a fuss.

There's a lot of hand-wringing going on at present.
But like most things it's just history repeating itself.
Over a century ago the country went through an identical

bout of wowserism, when burgeoning opportunities for gambling, coupled with growing puritanism, threw politicians into a panic. The 1881 Gaming and Lotteries Act clamped down on uncontrolled gambling, including betting on racing and sports (walking races, called 'pedestrianism', and professional athletics were flourishing), lotteries, sweepstakes, cards, two-up, dice and games of chance.

Sound familiar? Substitute gaming machines, Lotto, Instant Kiwi, scratchies, casinos, the TAB, housie, internet and television gambling, and you have today's equivalent of the Victorian evils. Throw in political correctness, earnest do-gooders, a nanny government and the belief that one's personal weaknesses are somebody else's fault, and the result is the same: parliament brings in new laws to stem the naughtiness.

By and large the 1881 Act was a failure. Only a few betting activities were prosecuted, mainly when the working classes were involved. Chinese gaming dens were shut down, but gentlemen in clubs continued wagering on cards and billiards. Street bookmakers were too well organised to get caught. (On-course bookmaking was still legal, as was the newly introduced racecourse totalisator.)

As racing expanded rapidly towards the turn of the century, public anxiety deepened. Members of parliament were divided. Some were racehorse owners and racing club stewards; others were vehemently opposed to betting, bookmakers and totalisators. Churches, especially

Protestant ones, led the denunciation. (Catholics have never regarded gambling as inherently sinful.) The Presbyterians devoted whole issues of their journal, *Christian Outlook*, to the evils of gambling, while one of the most outspoken clergymen was Churchill Julius, Anglican Bishop of Christchurch (and later Archbishop of New Zealand). Ironically, some years later the bishop's son, George Julius, invented the automatic totalisator, which was adopted worldwide.

The Women's Christian Temperance Union got in on the act, trying to get the totalisator banned. It found an unlikely ally in the bookmaking fraternity, who realised the tote would cut into their profits. What narrowly saved the totalisator (and hence the future of racing in this country) was that a government totalisator tax – at first 1.5 percent – had been introduced. Politicians quickly saw a handsome, dependable stream of income to be tapped into. And increased. Eventually legislation in 1910 brought an end to legal bookmaking, both on- and off-course, but it would be 40 years before the TAB (Totalisator Agency Board) was established. Meanwhile, bookies simply filled the vacuum by going underground, turning over millions of pounds each year as racing boomed.

Without betting, you don't have racing. Not on any significant scale, anyway. An exception is Dubai, where the sport is privately financed by the enormously wealthy ruling family. There are still several states in the USA where betting is prohibited and no formal racing industry exists. Funnily enough, until recently Texas, despite its association with horses, cowboys and the wild west, was one of them.

Before the totalisator was invented, you could bet on horses only through bookmakers, sweepstakes or private wagers. Then around 1865 a clever Parisian shop owner and punter named Pierre Oller thought up the *pari mutuel* (meaning 'mutual wager') system. Unhappy with the odds bookmakers were offering, he decided to run his own scheme. He sold tickets at the same price on horses in each race. From total money collected he deducted five percent commission, and distributed the rest among winning ticket holders in proportion to the number of tickets sold. Thus the public effectively set the odds, instead of the bookmaker.

Oller's idea was such a success that Parisian racetrack owners copied it. Soon this early form of totalisator replaced bookies in France entirely. Eventually all racing countries adopted a form of totalisator betting, although some retained bookmakers alongside the 'tote'. Some, notably Britain and Australia, still do. In New Zealand, bookmakers controlled betting until 1880, when the first crude, manually operated totalisator was used at the Canterbury Jockey Club. This was essentially just a device to record bets and adjust odds, and when the Auckland Racing Club used it later that year its shortcomings became evident. *The New Zealand Herald* reported: 'The totalisator was supposed to regulate betting, to renovate racing morals, and to render cheating impossible. The machine would appear, however, to open a wide door for nefarious transactions.'

What had happened was that four men who had backed a winner, King Quail, found their dividend had been shortened from the promised £12 to £3. In the subsequent court case, the tote operators claimed 'there had been a great run on King Quail after the horses started', and thus there were 14 investors, not four. The magistrate did not believe them, and they were sentenced to a month's hard labour.

Despite such an inauspicious start, the totalisator (with improvements to prevent fraud) continued to be used at Auckland's Ellerslie racetrack, and various forms, many extremely rudimentary, were introduced by other clubs. Patrons, however, remained deeply suspicious and it was a long while before the contraptions were widely accepted.

In the very old days, you could bet on horses only to win. Then bookmakers introduced second-place dividends, and eventually third-place – when there were enough runners. When the New Zealand TAB began operations in 1951, it offered the same bets. The government's intention was to *permit* legal off-course betting, not *encourage* it. TABs were not permitted to advertise, or to have more than one small, discreet sign. They could not provide seating (encouraging 'loitering'), or radio broadcasts, or any information (such as jockeys' names) that might assist bettors. Payouts could not be made on the same day, and bets had to be placed an hour and a half before the race. Tickets were written out by hand, in triplicate. Despite all this, punters came in droves. At the main Auckland outlet the opening hours were extended to the evening, and police had to be called to control the queues and break up fist fights.

Gradually attitudes softened, and 25 years after it began the TAB introduced some new types of bets, beginning with quinellas and trebles. These days you can bet on numerous sports as well as racing (and combine them in 'multi' bets). You can take doubles, trebles, quinellas, trifectas, 'Pick 6' (winners of six races) or a 'Six Pack' (the first six home in one race). You can have 'All Up' bets (your winnings are automatically transferred on to your next selected event); percentage bets (you get an equivalent percentage of the dividend); take fixed odds on certain races, and probably a whole lot more I've forgotten. If all else fails, you can take an 'Easybet' – a lucky dip, chosen by the computer – which is often the source of the biggest payouts.

The most dramatic innovation in its history is just around the corner for the TAB. In 2005 it will introduce betting pools combined with those of other countries, starting with Australia. This will allow punters access to far bigger pools, often with far bigger dividends. Imagine it: the joy of backing Kiwi horses at Aussie odds ...

... and how
to bet

IF YOU LOST the plot in that last section, don't worry. I will now explain in simple terms how to place a bet. I am assuming you are new to this, and not such a wuss you will make others do it for you.

The first thing to learn is to use numbers, not names. A tip: the number of the runner is the big one to the left of the name, not the smaller one in brackets (that's its 'barrier draw', the position it starts from). Do not worry about deciphering race books: they are now so complicated they might as well be written in Sanskrit. Actually most tote operators will help you out if you do say a name, because they'll realise you're a novice – but it takes longer, and you're trying not to look like a beginner, aren't you?

Then you have to know *where* you want to bet, and on what race. If you're at the races, the operator will assume you want a bet on the next event there, but at a TAB you need to tell them which meeting you want. There will always be several choices. (Note, this does not apply on Melbourne Cup day, when they'll assume you only want to bet on that one race.) You also need to know how much you want to bet, and on what kind of bet. (For a detailed explanation of bet types, see pages 74–78.)

So let's pretend you're at the races and you've sorted out your fancy. You really like Phar Lap, and look, he's number 1 in the next race. Probably worth a couple of dollars each way. You go up to the tote window and say, 'Two dollars each way on number 1, please.' Hand over your $4, and you'll be given a ticket with all that information on it, including the runner's name. Don't lose your ticket! When Phar Lap romps home, let's say paying $20 to win and $7 for a place, you take your ticket back to the tote and they'll give you $54.

Well, most of that is true. Of course Phar Lap is dead, and he would never have paid that much anyway. But even if you win only a small amount, it will seem a lot. The good thing about winning money at the races is that it is worth far more than other types of money. And if you go home breaking even, you've still won, because you've had a whole day out that's cost you nothing. Where else can you do that?

Here are a few other handy hints. These apply to all punters, not just beginners.

- Never change your mind while you're waiting to put a bet on. Your first choice will always come in — especially when you've marked it in your race book.

- If you accidentally get the wrong ticket, never ask to cancel it, although it's okay to take your original bet as well, as insurance. The accidental bet usually comes in.

- If your bet is a complicated one (for example, you're taking several horses in a trifecta), it is a good idea to fill in a betting form beforehand. This is better for the people in the queue behind you. It's also good for shy people, because you don't have to say anything when you place your bet.

- Don't throw your ticket away immediately after the race just because you didn't win. Sometimes there are protests, and unplaced runners are promoted into a dividend-bearing place. It is most unbecoming to be seen scrabbling around on your hands and knees looking for a discarded tote ticket.

- Try not to borrow money to bet with, but if you do always pay your debts as soon as possible, even if your last-gasp hope has lost. (This is the origin of the phrase 'paying off a dead horse'.)

- Never try to talk someone out of their choice. I once did this to my niece, and the horse paid $25 for a place. Fortunately, she was too young to bear grudges.

- Do not bet more than you can cheerfully afford to lose, with the emphasis on cheerfully. Yes, I know this sounds like your granny, but there's nothing worse than a bad loser.

My mother's superior system

I N EARLIER TIMES it was quite common to have fortune tellers and other helpful guides on racecourses to help punters with their picks. A favourite was the trained canary, which for a fee would pick the winner of each race by selecting a card from a pack in its beak, and presenting it to the 'lucky' gambler. Monkeys hired from circuses were used in a similar manner. Such gimmicks are now frowned on, so you have to devise your own scheme to beat the odds.

Rather than concentrating on picking winners, a good plan is to concentrate on not having complete losses. You do this by having a system for betting and sticking to it.

And remember, any system — even the old pin through the race book — is better than no system at all.

There are three types of punters. You are either:

1   a complete beginner
2   partly knowledgeable, or
3   extremely knowledgeable or a professional punter.

I will not insult those in category 3 by attempting to tell them how to bet, and anyway they will not be reading this book. But here are some tips for groups 1 and 2.

COMPLETE BEGINNER

You are contemplating having a bet because you're in the TAB on Melbourne Cup day (see page 73). Or you're at the one meeting a year you attend — a summer picnic meeting such as Thames, Tauherenikau, Waikouaiti or Kurow, or the Auckland, Wellington or New Zealand Cup carnivals. You won't win every time (unless you're amazingly lucky) but to give yourself a better chance of winning occasionally, here are some methods:

Numbers   Choose a number from, say, 1 to 7. (Most fields have at least seven starters.) Stick to it and back it each way (that is, for a win and a place) in every race. Sooner or later that number will come in. It is also really easy to remember this bet — not a trifling matter at the end of a long, hot day in the sun or bar.

Jockeys   Choose a jockey (or driver — the ones sitting in carts) you like the sound of, preferably one featuring in most races (the good ones always do). If you are female, choose a woman (for solidarity, and they win lots of races anyway).

First sight If you're at the race meeting, have a look out on the track or in the birdcage, and note the first horse you see. Even if it's lying down having a rest, back it. This is not a systematic, logical bet like the others, but it provides great personal satisfaction when it occasionally works.

Greys If there's a grey horse, back it. Even if it doesn't win, at least you'll be able to see it throughout the race. If there are several greys back them all, as they will be indistinguishable.

Colours Pick your favourite colour and back whichever jockey or driver is wearing the most of it. Note that this entails scrutiny of all starters before each race, which can get rather tedious. Do not rely on descriptions in the race book – they're often difficult to comprehend. What bloke knows what 'eau de nil' or 'tangerine' is? And what's the difference between sashes, braces and hoops anyway?

PARTLY KNOWLEDGEABLE

By this I mean you can understand some of the jargon and symbols in the race book, have been to the races or TAB before, know the rudiments of betting, and have vaguely heard of some of the horses and/or jockeys/drivers.

You are in the happy position of being able to impress those around you with your superior knowledge. Tell them absolutely anything and they'll believe you. ('Of course all jockeys' whips are electrically charged.') And you will be able to explain convincingly why the horse you backed in the last race didn't win. Here are some suitable systems for you:

Fourths　Back any horse that ran fourth at its last start. If there are more than one, back them all. Fourth is a very good place to run at your last start, unless there were only four runners. It generally means the horse can improve, especially if it hasn't had many races lately.

Form　This next one's really good, but it involves a bit of working out, so it's best to do it before leaving home, which means buying a newspaper or turf guide. What you do is add up the figures in front of each horse's name. These tell you where they finished at their last few starts, known as their 'form'. A zero means they came in tenth or worse (so that counts as 10, not 0). Then divide by the number of starts, and back whichever horse has the smallest total.

If they've all had four starts, the smallest possible total is one (four firsts, divided by four). Ignore the little x and the dot in the form line – they just mean a break from racing of over four weeks (dot) or over three months (x). If the numbers won't divide evenly, just take a stab. After a while you'll quickly pick out the ones that will have the lowest score, and won't have to do the calculation for every single horse.

Winner two starts ago   Back a horse that won at its second-to-last start, and then came fifth or worse at its last. Note that this is in complete contradiction to the above two systems. The reasoning is that if it was good enough to win a couple of starts back it will probably do so again, and the last start failure means it will pay more. Also, it may have met with bad luck last time, and not many horses are consistently unlucky.

Newspaper tips   Follow the racing expert's tips in the newspaper. If there are several experts, just choose one. Couple up all this person's tips in boxed quinellas and trifectas. Being a partly knowledgeable person, you'll know how to do this. Stick with their selections right to the end, and if you don't win at all write a rude letter of complaint to the paper.

Appearance   If you're at the course, watch the horses as they walk around the birdcage. Back the one that has the shiniest coat and prances around, taking tiny little steps, as if it can't wait to race. You do, however, have to be able to distinguish between shining and sweating, and you don't want it to overdo the prancing or it'll be wasting too much energy.

A slight drawback is that lots of horses prance. And sometimes the ones that wander around yawning end up winning. Roodyvoo, whom I always backed, used to amble around with his head hanging down, and if he had to wait for too long in the starting stalls he'd fall asleep. Yet he won lots of races. On second thoughts, this tip might be one for the 'extremely knowledgeable' group.

Winter special   Find out which sires consistently produce horses that like soft or heavy going. An example is Starjo: always back his offspring when the track's heavy, whatever their form. Compile a list from past results – it's surprising how often it works. And when you think about it, surprising *why* it works. It's mainly to do with foot size, dinner plates not sinking in as far as dainty little hooves. As someone who used to test racetrack surfaces by seeing how far my high heels went in (before going on the radio to tell punters), I can vouch for this theory.

There is in fact a fourth group of punters, of which my mother was one. I would call this the 'intuitive' category. Mum was Irish and her father had been a sea captain, therefore she chose horses with Irish or sea-connected names. There are a lot of these. This may be because so many racehorse owners have Irish blood, which, as everybody knows, carries the gambling gene.

But don't think, if you belong to this group, that you must be consistent. For no apparent reason my mother would back a horse named Blue Blade or Anacapri. She picked up £68 when Blue Blade ran third in the 1963 Wellington Cup, and got the Anacapri–Shamrock Queen double that paid over £5,000. Intuition is all very well, but you must know when to ignore it.

Forty excuses for your horse not winning

OWNER 'Why didn't you take that gap at the top of the straight?'

JOCKEY 'Because the gap was going faster than the bloody horse.'

Hoary old stories like this are still heard on racetracks. But there are many more convincing reasons why your horse may not win. In the days when telegrams were the quickest and cheapest method of communication, a famous American owner had numerous horses trained in various states by various trainers. He knew all the reasons (excuses) his horses hadn't won, and to save on telegraph bills sent the trainers a numbered list to use when reporting results. He got them to quote numbers only, as if they were ordering a Chinese meal.

The list has been expanded since then. It is useful not only for trainers and owners but for you, the punter, especially if you like to give tips to others. You may like to copy the list and carry it about with you, to be surreptitiously consulted when necessary. For the sake of convenience, I've used the male gender. Adapt if the horse is female.

1 Your horse broke down during the race.

2 Your horse died during the race.

3 Your horse was knocked off its feet by another runner. (With dogs this happens all the time.)

4 The jockey fell off.

5 Your horse wouldn't go into the barrier, and they scratched him. (i.e. I hadn't given him enough practice at getting used to the starting gates.)

6 The track was too heavy/soft/easy/firm.

7 If heavy, your horse got bogged down; if firm, it 'jarred up'. If in between, it 'just didn't handle the going'.

8 Your horse didn't see out the distance.

9 The race was too short – he's crying out for extra ground.

10 Have you considered trying him as a jumper?

11 That big roomy track/narrow turning track didn't suit him.

12 Your horse got boxed in on the rails.

13 Your horse was wide the whole way.

14 The pace was too fast up front.

15 They dawdled the first half and he couldn't sprint at the end.

16 Your horse was held up for a run in the straight.

17 A gap opened up, but your horse wouldn't go through it.

18 The gap closed.

19 The jockey/driver took him to the front too soon.

20 The jockey/driver left his run too late.

21 Your horse never had a chance from that wide draw.

22 That inside draw didn't suit his style of running.

23 Your horse shied at a shadow on the track/somebody standing by the inside rail.

24 Your horse needs a stronger jockey.

25 The jockey didn't follow my instructions.

26 Your horse was too fresh – he needed the race.

27 Your horse needs a spell.

28 Your horse was in season (applies only to female horses).

29 I think we'll have to cut him (applies only to young male horses, and means the horse should be gelded). This is because he's too interested in female horses, too aggressive, is 'pinching himself' (his testicles are getting in the way), or is too much trouble for the trainer. Generally the last.

30 The handicapper crucified him. (He couldn't carry the weight allotted.)

31 The company was a bit rich. (I talked you into racing him out of his class.)

32 Your horse got his tongue over the bit.

33 He choked on a clod of dirt.

34 He's much better the other way round (meaning, if a right-handed track, he prefers left-handed ones, and vice versa).

35 Your horse pulled too hard. I think I'll try him in blinkers.

36 Your horse didn't like racing in blinkers.

37 The saddle slipped. (I didn't do it up tight enough.)

38 The bridle broke. (I've been saving money by using old gear.) Excellent for trotters, who have much more gear to break.

39 Your horse finished first, but he was too wide out and the judge didn't see him. (This happened in the past, but not since photo finishes were invented.)

40 We wuz robbed.

Plus some extra excuses for dogs:

1 Your dog got into a fight.

2 Your dog was shunted right off the track.

3 Your dog did a somersault in his box, and was facing the wrong way at the start. (This happened to my dog once.)

4 The dogs caught the bunny (electrically operated lure) and the race was abandoned.

5 The bunny wouldn't work and the whole meeting was abandoned.

So it's
Melbourne
Cup day

OKAY. SO IT'S the first Tuesday in November. The race that stops two nations has come around again and you're down at the TAB, surrounded by people who look as if they know what they're doing. Be assured, a lot of them don't. You, on the other hand, armed with the knowledge you've picked up in this book, are ready to have a bet.

Now what kind of bet will you choose? One of the great things about the Melbourne Cup is that the TAB knows plenty of people are once-a-year punters, and does all it can to make it simple for you. Some of the bigger TABs even have special staff whose job it is to walk around looking for people with bewildered expressions.

But there is no need for you to look bewildered. Here's what you do. First, decide on a horse you like the sound of. Follow your instincts. Pick the name that jumps off the page at you. My neighbour had a nice little windfall backing Rogan Josh in 1999 — because she'd enjoyed the dish at a restaurant the week before.

Don't be talked out of your pick. A TAB colleague won on Saintly in 1996 because the trainer, Bart Cummings, was the only name he recognised. (Cummings has won a record 11 Cups.) He wisely ignored my advice that, with its breeding, Saintly would not stay the distance.

Then decide how much you want to spend. Think about how much you can afford to lose. The price of a coffee? A lunch? A new pair of shoes? Or just a dollar? Do not bet more than you'd mind losing.

Next decide what kind of bet you're going to have. Here are the main choices, starting with the simplest:

Win   Your selection has to come first. (If it's a dead heat, that counts as a win.) The minimum you can bet is $1. *Always the choice of the super-confident.*

Place   Your selection has to run first, second or third. You won't get as big a dividend as on a win bet, but you have three times as many chances. Again, the minimum bet is $1. *Good if you are of timid temperament.*

Each Way This combines a win and place bet. It gives you the chance of a big win dividend, with the insurance of still getting a payout if your horse finishes only second or third. The minimum you can spend is $2. (You ask for 'a dollar each way'.) A really good trick is to put *more* for a place (say $1 to win, $3 for a place), which means you'll still make a profit even if your horse gets only second or third. Betting like this is not going to make you a fortune, but think how you'll be able to skite about it for the rest of the year. *Absolutely ideal for the cautious.*

Quinella A good bet if you can't make up your mind between two horses. They have to run first and second (in either order) for you to collect. Again, you only have to spend $1. *Great for waverers.*

Boxed Quinella To give yourself a better chance of winning a quinella, you can take more than two runners and 'box' them. Say you pick three horses. In a 'boxed quinella', if any two run first and second (in either order) you collect, and you've spent just $3. Of course you can box more than three, but be careful to check how much this will cost, as the amount increases with each additional runner. For example, four horses boxed will cost $6, and five will be $10. *Even better – you can waver all over the place.*

Trifecta   To win a trifecta, you have to pick three horses to run first, second and third in the correct order. That's fairly difficult. If you succeed, you'll get a nice fat dividend for your $1 – usually in the thousands, especially on big races like the Melbourne Cup. *For the optimist.*

Boxed Trifecta   As with a quinella, you have a better chance of winning a trifecta if you 'box' your choices. That way, your three horses can finish first, second and third in any order. This will cost $6 instead of $1, but you can also take 50-cent units, making your outlay only $3. The more horses you take, the better your chances, but the cost rises sharply with each additional runner. For example, four horses boxed will cost $24 (or $12 for 50-cent units).* *For the cautious optimist.*

Double   This involves picking the winners of two different specified races (they're called the first leg and second leg). Mostly these are 'concession' doubles, which means if the horse you've chosen in the first leg wins,

---

* I hesitate to mention this, not wanting to confuse you if you're a beginner, but the TAB has introduced what it calls 'percentage betting', applying to trifectas, trebles and a couple of complicated bets. Essentially what this means is you can take even smaller units (as little as 5 cents), although you have to spend a minimum of $5. So you can couple up many more runners for the same outlay, but of course your dividend is proportionately smaller.

your second-leg horse can run either first or second (but if second, you get a smaller dividend). *For thinking types – you need to think about two races, not just the Cup.*

Treble   A treble is like a double, but is harder, because you have to pick the winners of three specified races. And there is no 'concession' treble. Doubles and trebles are both $1 bets – however, if you want to take more than one horse in each leg, you can bet in 50-cent units, though you have to spend a minimum of $2. *For those with even greater attention span.*

Easybet   As the name implies, this is ideal for those who can't make up their minds or can't be bothered to think about it at all. The computer picks the horses. All you have to decide is how much you want to spend, and on what kind of bet. (If you don't specify, you'll get a trifecta.) You can take each-way (minimum $2), quinella or trifecta Easybets (both minimum $3). There are plenty of people who've had big collects from their $3 Easybets on Cup day, and not a cent back from their own selections. *For the lazy, uncommitted, bewildered, and everyone (including me) who has last-minute doubts about their own choices.*

Big Race Pack   This is a Melbourne Cup special, kindly provided by the TAB, that combines an Easybet with your own each-way bet. For $10, you choose a horse, and the computer picks the others to combine in a quinella and trifecta, in addition to $3 each way on your selection. *Here you have the best of both worlds: a bet to appeal to the cautious and the optimistic. After all, if you're only going to bet once a year, you may as well aim for the sky.*

Now you know how to bet, you may want to consider another method of picking your horse, beyond the name that catches your eye. Experts who've been studying the Melbourne Cup for years have various theories, and there are always statistics to fall back on. For instance, four- and five-year-olds win more Cups than other age groups. Number 1 (the topweight) has not won since 1954, although is quite often placed. Lightweights — say numbers 18 onwards — seldom win (although Brew, number 24, did in 2000) but often sneak into a place, lifting trifecta dividends.

Mares don't win nearly as often as male horses, mainly because not as many start. In the race's 143-year history, only 14 females have won. But Jezabeel, Ethereal and Makybe Diva — all mares — have won three of the last six Cups, proving the unreliability of statistics. New Zealand-breds have won 40 times, 35 since 1947, and numbers 4 and 12 are the luckiest, each having had 11 wins.

One system I always consider is the outcome of certain lead-up races, such as the Caulfield Cup, run about three weeks beforehand, and the Mackinnon Stakes, run the Saturday prior. The theory is simple: for a horse to see out the tough, 3,200-metre Melbourne Cup, it needs to be at peak fitness. If it's good enough to finish in, say, the first four of either of these other races (which always attract classy fields), then chances are it's fit enough.

The problem with this theory is that not all Melbourne Cup runners start in either of those races. In recent years, Northern Hemisphere trainers have been bringing horses to Australia and not following the traditional pattern. As a rule, European horses are raced much less frequently than 'down under' horses. And remember our own idol, Kiwi? When he won in that dazzling last-to-first burst in 1983, it was his first outing in Australia. Farm-trained by his owner Snow Lupton, Kiwi arrived in Melbourne only a few days before the Cup, and was virtually ignored by the pundits.

Which is part of the great charm of the Melbourne Cup. With prize-money of several million dollars (AU$4,600,000 in 2004) it is the world's richest handicap race, yet it can be won by the humblest of horses (and owners). The key is that word 'handicap'. Although handicap races have been around for centuries, racing purists look down their noses at them. This is because theoretically they give every horse a chance of winning, with the worst horse getting the lightest weight and the best the heaviest. The 'true test' of a horse is to win at equal weights against the same age group. Or under the standard weight-for-age scale, among horses of different ages and sex. None of the other great international races – the English and Kentucky Derbys, the Prix de l'Arc de Triomphe, the Japan Cup, the Breeders' Cup in the USA and the Dubai World Cup – are handicaps.

Many great champions, such as Rising Fast, Tulloch and Kingston Town, have been beaten because of their hefty handicaps. Rising Fast's was a remarkable case. He had won the 1954 Melbourne and Caulfield Cups, and in 1955 won the Caulfield again, so his allotted weight of 10 stone (63.5 kilograms) in that year's Melbourne Cup was well earned. But he just failed to catch fellow New Zealander Toparoa, who was carrying 38 pounds (15.5 kilograms) less. Nobody would ever suggest that Rising Fast was an inferior horse to Toparoa.

Let's face it, the Melbourne Cup, despite its critics, is simply a unique phenomenon. Since 1993, when Vintage Crop became the first Northern Hemisphere-trained horse to succeed, some of the world's wealthiest owners have tried to win it – and so far failed. The State of Victoria recognises Cup day with a public holiday. The rest of Australia, and most of New Zealand, stops work for it, and many people take the afternoon off to attend Melbourne Cup parties. Practically every workplace runs a sweepstake. Conversations in days ahead begin, 'Who do you like in the Cup?' It is not just sporting news. You would have to live in total seclusion to be unaware of it.

Every year New Zealanders bet more, by a margin of millions, on this Australian race than on any run in their own country.

The race has been held since 1861 on Melbourne's Flemington racecourse, named after Bob Fleming, a local butcher of the time. The number of starters has ranged from a low of seven in 1863 to a high of 39 in Carbine's year, 1890. Today the maximum is 24.

Almost every Cup has its drama, and occasional tragedies, beginning with the inaugural race, when two of the 17 starters fell and had to be destroyed. Back then 4,000 people made their way to Flemington and voted the event a raging success. These days the crowd regularly reaches 100,000, and the carnival atmosphere almost overshadows the racing. Yet when the race was first mooted a contemporary newspaper journalist poured scorn on the idea of a two-mile, handicap event.

'Its effect,' he wrote, 'would be to make any brumby bought out of a mob for thirty shillings the equal of the finest horse in the land ... It is a mad idea, doomed to failure.'

Now there was someone who couldn't pick a winner!

Some juicy racing scandals

WHEREVER LARGE amounts of money are at stake, corruption lurks around the corner. Racing and gambling have always co-existed, and scandals are part of racing's colourful history. But as a shrewd observer once said, 'To be successful as a scoundrel on the turf, a man must either work single-handed, or must have accomplices who are deaf, dumb, unable to write and without any memory.'

These days scams are far less frequent, largely eliminated by videotaping of races, photo finishes, drug testing and strict law enforcement.

But this is not to say new ones won't be invented. The 2004 'blue magic' scandal involved a previously undetectable drug. Likewise, betting exchanges (where, through a kind of internet stock exchange system, punters can actually make money on horses or dogs that lose) make use of today's technology. Both are essentially cheating – or, in the latter case, encouraging cheating – and will surely be stamped out. But inevitably something else will take their place, and honest racing people (by far the majority) will suffer.

Look Out   A highly publicised trotting scandal of the 1920s led to New Zealand harness racing cleaning up its act. Prior to this, ring-ins (substitution of one horse for another) were fairly common, and many doubtless went undetected. Two factors contributed to the problem. First, bookmakers, although banned, were flourishing in the absence of any legal off-course betting, and big money could be won. Second, trotters were then handicapped according to their winning times, so drivers often held back horses for a slower time, or deliberately did not win.

Taking advantage of the rules, 'Look Out' won a mile-and-a-half trot at Invercargill in 1924 in average time. This netted a large haul from bookies, but an even bigger haul was made when he started from the front mark against a better field the next day, and again won easily.

Unfortunately, the real Look Out's former owner read of these wins, and contacted trotting authorities, pointing out that his horse could not possibly have improved so much. Further investigation suggested that this same horse (by then impounded) had also, under the name Eulius, won at a Poverty Bay meeting the year before. Coincidentally, Eulius's trainer had also trained the high-class Willie Lincoln, top stake earner of 1920–21. He had no difficulty recognising Willie Lincoln as both 'Eulius' and 'Look Out'. All the swindling parties were sent to prison and disqualified from trotting for life.

Fine Cotton   A now legendary Australian scandal in 1984 involved a ring-in galloper named Fine Cotton, trained by former New Zealander Hayden Haitana. As an attempt at pulling off a major betting coup, the Fine Cotton plan had all the subtlety of the Keystone Kops. The real Fine Cotton was a poorly performed eight-year-old brown gelding with no white markings. The horse impersonating him was the somewhat more talented Bold Personality, a seven-year-old bay with white feet and a star on his forehead. Bold Personality was bandaged to conceal his leg markings, and his coat coloured with brown hair dye.

But as 'Fine Cotton' passed the post a narrow winner, the Eagle Farm stewards had already smelt a rat. Alerted to the heavy off-course betting that had brought the horse's price down from 33–1 to 7–2 equal favourite, and suspicious of the excuse given by Haitana when he failed to produce the horse's registration papers, they lodged an appeal and awarded the race to the second-placed Harbour Gold.

An estimated $2 million stood to be won if the scam had worked. Prominent Sydney bookmaker Robbie Waterhouse and his father Bill were among those implicated and barred from racetracks for up to 15 years. Meanwhile, Hayden Haitana did a runner, but was found after a fortnight and served a jail term, as did the so-called mastermind, used car salesman John 'The Phantom' Gillespie.

Running Rein Substituting one horse for another is, of course, one of the oldest tricks in the book, but not many people have the gall to try it in the most important race on the calendar, the English Derby. What's more, it worked – until the case went to court, and 'Running Rein' (actually a four-year-old named Maccabaeus) was disqualified, and the second horse, Orlando, made the official winner of the 1844 Derby. Perhaps the most extraordinary fact about this most famous of English racing scandals is that the stewards allowed the horse to start, even though they had been told he was a four-year-old. (The Derby is open only to three-year-olds.) They decided that if he won they would withhold the stakes, pending an inquiry. Chaos over betting settlements raged after the race, and 'Running Rein's owner, Goodman Levy, fled the course and later the country.

Tregonwell Frampton   This imposingly named professional horseman had enormous prestige as 'Keeper of the royal running horses at Newmarket' to five successive monarchs. After the death of Charles II and before the evolution of the Jockey Club, he adjudicated racing disputes and generally ran the whole caboodle.

He was also a fearless gambler, quite happy to bet £1,000 (about a million in today's currency) on a race. And he was none too scrupulous. Accepting a challenge from a prominent Yorkshire owner to run their horses in a match race – two runners only – Frampton instructed his groom to persuade the groom of the challenging horse to arrange a secret trial. This was supposed to be at the weights assigned for the match proper, but Frampton's horse, on his instructions, carried seven pounds more. When the other horse won by only a length, Frampton was certain his horse would win at even weights, so plunged heavily. But it transpired that the other horse's groom had informed his master of the intended secret trial, and that wily owner had decided to exploit it to his own advantage by putting another seven pounds on his horse. Thus when the official match race was run, the two horses finished in the same order, separated by a length.

Many of Frampton's friends who had backed his horse faced bankruptcy. The extent of the losses and the amount of property changing hands provoked the English parliament into enacting a law in 1710 to inhibit excessive betting – not that it had any effect.

George North   In 1881 Wellington was rocked by a scandal involving sweepstake king George North. 'Calcutta sweeps' were then a popular form of betting, with thousands of pounds invested with organisers, who were usually publicans or barbers. Big races, including the Melbourne Cup, were chosen and advertisements were run inviting investors and outlining the prizes. North, who owned a Lambton Quay barber's shop, had been conducting such sweeps since 1874, always openly and honestly, and paying the generous prizes promptly. The draws for horses became well-attended social occasions, enhanced by the barber's gregarious and jovial nature.

For the 1881 Wellington Cup, North advertised in *The Evening Post* well in advance, offering total prize money of £4,000 for tickets costing £1 each. The advertisement included the words, 'Mr North's former racing sweeps have invariably been conducted with such thorough fairness as to give entire satisfaction to all interested, and we are not surprised to hear that there is already brisk demand for his "four thousand-pounder".'

But a nasty surprise was in store. A few weeks before the race, North caught a boat to San Francisco, taking all his subscribers' money with him. The affair knocked the stuffing out of the sweepstakes market, hastened the introduction of the 1881 Gaming and Lotteries Act, and vindicated those who had denounced sweepstakes as 'the most evil of the gambling mania that is now sweeping [!] the country'.

Some moderately interesting facts about racing

NEW ZEALAND is now a world leader in the number of female jockeys, yet it was one of the last countries to allow women to ride against men in official races. When Linda Jones led the charge in the mid 1970s, racing authorities declined her initial application for a licence on the grounds that she was too old (at 23), not strong enough, married, and might take away opportunities for male riders. The 1977 Human Rights Commission Act changed all that, and on 22 July the following year an apprentice named Sue Day became the first female New Zealand jockey to win a totalisator race here. (Canadian rider Joan Phipps had won the previous November under a special licence.) Female apprentices now outnumber males, and women riders from around the world move to New Zealand to get the 'fair go' they are denied at home. Although other countries allowed women to ride earlier, prejudice against them remains strong. In New Zealand nobody bats an eyelid when a woman jockey wins a major race: they do it so often. In places like Australia it would still be big news.

SOME PEOPLE complain that there are too many clubs and too much racing in New Zealand these days. But back in 1883 there were 194 racing or trotting clubs listed in the Turf Register, and no fewer than 40 race meetings were held on Boxing Day (and even one on Christmas Day).

IT IS A LITTLE-KNOWN fact that the great Ngati Toa warrior chief Te Rauparaha took an interest in racing – at least that's the conclusion you can draw from Sir William Fox's *Six Colonies of New Zealand*. Describing Te Rauparaha's final days, when he had a missionary among his many bedside visitors, Fox writes that after the missionary left, Te Rauparaha 'turned the conversation to the Whanganui races, where one of his guests had been running a horse'. Since Te Rauparaha died on 27 November 1849, and Wanganui's second annual race meeting, organised by the military, had been held on 6 and 7 November, this account rings true.

WHEN RACING began in England, horses were at least five or six years old, and carried big weights over long distances. Gradually ages and weights came down, and even yearlings were raced, although this was officially banned in 1860. Today horses must be two years old before they are allowed to race.

NEW ZEALAND has always permitted women to train their own racehorses, but the first woman licensed to train on behalf of others was Granny McDonald in 1924. When one of Granny's charges, Catalogue, contested (and won) the 1938 Melbourne Cup, she had to send her husband with the horse, as Australia prohibited women trainers. Australian newspapers mentioned the 'unprecedented combination of woman owner and woman trainer' (Catalogue's owner was Mrs Tui Jamieson), and prime minister Michael Joseph Savage was among many to send Granny a congratulatory telegram.

In 2001 another woman trainer from New Zealand won the Melbourne Cup with Ethereal (in fact she went one better, winning the Caulfield Cup as well). But by then female trainers were permitted in Australia, so Sheila Laxon is in the record book as creating an historic first.

IN THE HORSEY world you're not called a half-brother or half-sister unless you have the same mum. Dads don't count. That's because stallions can leave literally thousands of offspring, while mares are lucky to produce a dozen.

MANY NON-RACING people think using whips on horses is cruel. In fact, the 'windmill' action used by most New Zealand riders looks worse than it really is: often it's a brushing rather than hitting action, in rhythm with the horse's stride. And from the horse's point of view, there's a big difference between a whack when you're standing still and a whack when you're galloping flat out with adrenaline flowing – as any contact sports player knows. Jockeys can be fined or suspended for 'excessive use of the whip', and stipendiary stewards and veterinarians have to report any breaches of the rule.

THE DERBY, or variations of it, is the most important race for three-year-olds everywhere, but it could easily have been called the 'Bunbury'. Sir Charles Bunbury and his fellow racing enthusiast the twelfth Earl of Derby dreamed up the idea of the race during one of many rollicking parties at the latter's house. They tossed a coin to decide what it should be called, and Derby won. Ironically, Bunbury's horse Diomed won the inaugural Derby in 1780. The previous year the pair had also founded The Oaks, a similar race for fillies, named after Lord Derby's house.

A PROMINENT English racehorse born in 1773 was called Pot-8-Os – or Potooooooo, as the illiterate (or early text-messaging) stable-hand spelt it on the stable door. Belying his unglamorous name, Potoooooooo turned out to be an excellent runner, winning 30 of his 48 races, and became the key figure in continuing the overwhelmingly dominant Darley Arabian male line, through his father Eclipse and son Waxy, to the present day.

UNLIKE MANY racing terms, 'steeplechase' was originally what it says: a race in a more or less straight line between two steeples, visible from a distance, and over whatever obstacles came in the way. The first recorded race took place in 1752, when two Irishmen rode between the churches of Buttevant and St Leger in County Cork. The sport gradually caught on in England, but the revolutionary idea of racing over a circular, well-marked course for the benefit of spectators didn't occur until 1830. And while England established the most famous steeplechase of them all, the Grand National at Aintree, Liverpool, Irish-bred horses have won it around 75 percent of the time since it began in 1839.

THE MOST FORMIDABLE of the English Grand National's many scary fences is Becher's Brook. The name commemorates a leading amateur rider of the time, Captain Becher, whose horse fell at the water-filled ditch during the inaugural event. It is claimed Becher emerged from the ditch declaring that water without brandy tasted even nastier than he had imagined.

AMERICA'S MARYLAND Hunt Cup, first run in 1894, is one of the world's most highly rated steeplechases, and one of the oddest. The four-mile event is contested over private farmland, the ground is uneven, with patches of 30-centimetre-high grass in places, and most of the fences are of the upright, five-bar, solid wood variety — totally unforgiving. Winners automatically qualify for entry in the English Grand National. The race regularly attracts over 15,000 spectators. There is no (official) betting, and no other events on the day.

AN AMERICAN jockey called Tod Sloan changed the way riders rode in races. Until his arrival in England in 1897, jockeys sat upright, with long stirrups. Sloan used short stirrups and a crouched stance, leaning forward behind the horse's head to reduce wind resistance. He was at first roundly ridiculed, but when he began winning so many races his 'monkey on a stick' position was adopted by the other jockeys, and eventually spread worldwide. It's claimed Sloan first used the position when a horse bolted and he pulled up his knees to get a better hold. This redistributed his weight, allowing the horse to stride out while he gained greater control. He then perfected the technique by studying bareback black riders in quarter-horse races.

FOR A HORSE to be grey in colour, it must have at least one grey parent. Note, however, that two greys will not automatically produce a grey foal; their foals may be any colour. If the grey colour skips a generation, it is lost. This makes it all the more remarkable that all grey thoroughbreds trace back more than 300 years to an early Arab import into England, the Alcock Arabian. Occasionally horses are registered as chestnut or bay because that's how they look when they're born, but as they age it becomes evident they are grey. In New Zealand the stallion Three Legs was originally registered as a bay, but he kept siring grey offspring from non-grey mares, so eventually his colour was corrected in the Stud Book.

STANDARDBREDS are more uniform in colour than thoroughbreds. Most are bay or brown, with few chestnuts and even fewer greys. Even rarer are skewbalds (large brown and white patches). The one family extant in New Zealand goes back to Snowflake, a trotting sensation of the 1940s. Snowflake was sensational not only for her striking appearance, but because she was the best staying three-year-old of her time. Her skewbald colouring traced to a pony stallion imported for show and breeding purposes, so she was not a 'pure' standardbred. Snowflake passed on the skewbald *and* piebald (black and white patches) colour to many of her descendants, but none – including the most recent, Splashed – has ever approached her quality.

ALTHOUGH GREY standardbreds are rare, two rank as legends. One was the American-bred gelding Greyhound, who won 71 races and at one time held 14 world records. His record for trotting a mile in 1.55.25 minutes stood from 1938 to 1969. The other was the mare Lady Suffolk. In 1845, aged 12, she became the first trotter to pull a wagon a mile in under 2.30. She raced for an incredible 16 years, and unsurprisingly her form tapered off as she reached her twenties. She was immortalised in the American folk-song 'The Old Grey Mare' (she ain't what she used to be ...).

BLUE IS THE term used to describe greyhounds with coats from pale grey to dark steely grey. So, perversely, there is no such thing as a grey greyhound. You also get 'blue' brindles, but of course they are not really blue either. Similarly, in horses, brown is the official description for what to most people looks black. True blacks are uncommon: they must have no brown hairs, even around the muzzle. A bay can be anything from pale tan to dark brown – the term really means a pattern. Bays always have black manes and tails, and usually black markings on the bottom part of their legs.

HARNESS HORSES, especially hoppled pacers (the ones with straps around their legs), wear so much gear it takes ages to get them dressed and undressed. Just as well they're placid. Moreover, trainers change their minds about what works and what doesn't, and every gear change has to be notified to the public.

Here's a random selection from one meeting: add undercheck; remove boring pole; add rein bar and murphy blind; add go straights; remove dexter ring bit, add regular bit; add half-blinds; add hopple shorteners; remove pull-up blinds; remove wire overcheck bit; add rearing strap; remove snaffle bit and earplugs; add nose flap; remove front bell boots, add figure eight; add pull-down half-blinds; add bandages and side strap; add steering corrector; remove rein pricker; add knee boot suspenders (just don't ask).

IN JUMPING races, the animals naturally have to clear the hurdles, but if another competitor has knocked them down it's perfectly okay to go through the fallen bit. Few have taken advantage of this rule as brazenly as the early runner Minnie Athol, competing in a hurdle race against two other starters at the Tararu course, Thames, in 1871. According to a contemporary report, Minnie 'just couldn't jump at all'. So her rider sat quietly near each jump and waited until one of the other horses (who obviously weren't much better) knocked it down. Then he rode her through the gap, caught up with the field, and waited at the next hurdle for the same thing to happen. To the delight of the crowd, Minnie Athol won the race. The other two riders lodged a protest, but the placings stood because no rule had been broken.

Some unusual characters of the turf

ECCENTRICITY HAS always been admired in England, home of racing, and throughout the world the sport has had its share of unusual characters, both human and equine. Here are a few notable examples:

Dorothy Paget One of my favourites of racing's many glorious old English eccentrics is Dorothy Paget. Born in 1905 into a rich, aristocratic family, she devoted most of her life (and money) to breeding, racing and betting on horses. She was pathologically shy, largely through an aversion to men. To avoid having to speak to them, she surrounded herself with a bevy of female secretaries, who accompanied her to the races. Once, during World War II, her car broke down on the way to a race meeting, and she missed her race. Thereafter, despite petrol rationing, she ordered a spare car to follow her whenever she went to a meeting.

A large, plain woman, with a pale round face, she always dressed for the races in an ankle-length grey over-coat and an old blue felt hat. Thanks to her strong will and perfectionist streak, she fell out regularly with her trainers, of whom there were many.

Towards the end of her life she became a recluse, and took to staying up all night, consuming vast meals, and sleeping during the day. This did not prevent her continuing to bet heavily (always on her own horses) and run her breeding and racing operations.

Although she spent huge sums attempting to get a Derby winner, her greatest success came as the owner of the champion steeplechaser Golden Miller, who won the 1934 Grand National, and the prestigious Cheltenham Gold Cup five times in succession.

Her most notable failure was Tuppence, who cost her 6,600 guineas as a yearling in 1931, the highest price of the Doncaster Sales. She insisted on giving this royally bred colt a plebeian name, despite warnings from experts. Tuppence eventually won £56 in a minor race, having failed dismally in the Derby, in which he was inexplicably the fourth favourite.

The Marquess of Hastings   Poor old Henry Hastings – not so much an eccentric as a disaster – was used by wealthy parents as an example of the dangers inherent in racing for young men with plenty of money and no sense. Described as 'attractive, idle, weak and spoiled', he turned from heavy drinking and gambling at cards to the race-track, where he began on a high note with his successful horse Lecturer. He won £70,000 on its first big race – it would have been far more if he hadn't been drunk when he made some of the bets.

Henry's best horse, Lady Elizabeth, kept him solvent after some disastrously big losses at the track, but he disgusted the racing world by continuing to race the filly long after she was obviously stale and tired.

With his fortune all but vanished, Henry fell into the clutches of a money lender and bookie's accomplice, who forced him to withdraw his favoured horse, The Earl, on the eve of the 1868 Derby. Instead, he ran the depleted Lady Elizabeth, who predictably finished down the track.

When he insisted on lining her up for The Oaks a couple of days later, the crowd hissed its disapproval. Henry died, broke and dissipated, a few months later, aged 26.

Lord Orford   Even by English eighteenth century standards, George, the third Earl of Orford, was regarded as an oddball. From a distinguished family – he was a grandson of prime minister Robert Walpole – he was said to use stags rather than horses to pull his carriage.

Orford squandered most of his family's wealth on his obsession with coursing (the forerunner to greyhound racing), breeding dogs and gambling on them. He used hundreds of dogs of different breeds in his experiments to increase the stamina of his greyhounds. With the English bulldog (then more like the bull terriers of today) he struck gold. After several generations of in-breeding, he achieved a smooth-haired dog that retained the sleek lines of the traditional greyhound but had additional power and courage. It also carried the gene for the bulldog's characteristic brindle colour.

Lord Orford's champion bitch Czarina – named soon after he sold his grandfather's priceless collection of paintings to Catherine the Great – is said to have won 47 consecutive match races. According to legend, Czarina brought about Orford's death. Unable to resist a challenge – and a large bet – Orford rose from his sickbed to witness her race, and fell from his horse, dead from a heart attack brought on by the excitement of her win.

However mad he was, Orford's part in the development of a superior racing greyhound has outlived him. Sceptics have cast doubt on his true contribution, but the incontrovertible fact of the brindle coat (previously greyhounds were black or white, or a mixture of both) has been confirmed by recent DNA evidence.

The Earl of Glasgow   Lord Glasgow was the breeder of Musket, sire of the great New Zealand champion Carbine. Not many people appreciated Lord Glasgow's good points (generosity to friends and occasional charity to the poor) because they were so greatly outweighed by his bad ones. He had a violent temper, and once set fire to a steward's bed at his club because the man had retired for the night and couldn't deliver him a whisky.

For 50 years, until his death in 1869, Glasgow bred and owned horses on a grand scale but had little success, winning only one classic, the 2000 Guineas in 1864. He treated his trainers and jockeys unpredictably and unfairly, but by far his most unpleasant trait was to order the execution, by shotgun, of any horses he deemed to be worthless — of which there were many.

This habit almost had a profound effect on New Zealand's racing history, for Musket was one of them. Musket's trainer, who saw the horse's potential, pleaded to save him, but the matter was unresolved when Lord Glasgow died suddenly. (Another version of this story is that the trainer shot a different horse of similar colour, and presented its ear, as per instructions, to his lordship.) All Glasgow's bloodstock was bequeathed to two friends, who ignored his order to carry on his practices. Musket turned out to be a good staying racehorse, and was exported to New Zealand in 1879, where he became the most influential sire of the nineteenth century.

Bella Button   New Zealand had its own celebrated
eccentric, Cantabrian Bella Button. An all-round horse-
woman, Bella was a champion showjumper, fearless
hunter, driver of six- and eight-in-hand pony teams, and
breaker-in of difficult horses. She won prizes – and a
regular income – in buck-jumping, the show-ring craze
of the late nineteenth century, and was a pioneer in the
racing industry.

In the early 1890s Bella trained, rode and drove her
own horses in official races against men, frequently beating them – until the South Island Trotting Association,
at its inaugural meeting in 1896, resolved 'that the rules
as adopted by the Trotting Associations north and south
do not contemplate the riding or driving of ladies...'
This rule would remain in place until 1979, two years
after the galloping code lifted its ban on women jockeys.

Bella could, however, continue to train her own
trotting horses, along with some steeplechasers. Her
father, who had encouraged her natural talents from the
start, bought a large estate in Christchurch that included
a full-sized racetrack – now the site of Queen Elizabeth
II Park – where she trained her horses. At 47, against the
advice of her family, the normally sensible Bella married
a man 16 years her junior. Gus Moore had a reputation
for 'indebtedness', and Bella would scare off bailiffs by
wielding a stockwhip at the gate. She was killed when
thrown from a horse outside her home in suburban New
Brighton, aged 57.

Carbine The great New Zealand-bred champion Carbine was an equine eccentric who gained a following akin to today's rock stars. He won 33 of his 43 starts, but his fame reached its peak when he won the 1890 Melbourne Cup carrying 10 stone 5 pounds (66 kilograms – still a record weight today) in record time. The stake money of over £10,000 – far more than the English Derby's – had attracted a high-class field of 39. 'Old Jack', as he was fondly known, received an ecstatic ovation. An historic photograph of the finish shows hats been thrown in the air and arms raised in elation. It was reported that grown men wept and strangers embraced in scenes of near hysteria.

Carbine had raced in Australia since he was three, and his idol status was partly due to his endearing idiosyncrasies, which were readily indulged. Highly intelligent (although not especially handsome, and with a clumsy walk), he used to stand stock still in the birdcage, gazing into the distance, waiting until he had sufficient applause and cheers from his crowd of admirers before deigning to move on to the track. He disliked getting his head wet, so his trainer designed a small umbrella-like contraption to fit over his ears on the way to the start in bad weather.

After four years at stud in Australia he was sold to the Duke of Portland for 13,000 guineas, more than twice the previous highest price for an Australasian stallion. The 'hat' went with him to England, where it was often needed.

Carbine's departure evoked an outpouring of emotion. Crowds gathered at railway stations along the route to the Melbourne wharf, where several thousand more waited to farewell him, many carrying floral tributes. As the ship left its berth, pandemonium erupted, and Carbine lifted his head, listening to the cheers for a final time.

Phar Lap   Seventy years after his death, Phar Lap is still a household name, and the racehorse against which others are measured in this part of the world. Although the Australians claim him as their own, Phar Lap was bred in New Zealand, and the racecourse near Timaru, his birthplace, is named after him. He has been the subject of several books and a full-length movie. And while he led an eventful life, even more unusual was his death and the public response to it.

Phar Lap never raced in New Zealand, and showed little promise in his first few starts in Australia. (I always remind people who want to give up early on a horse about this fact). But once he found form, he swept away all the opposition, and eventually won 37 of his 51 races, including 32 of his last 35. He was an exceptionally muscular horse with an outsize heart and a placid nature – which was just as well, as while walking to the Flemington track he was shot at by gangsters, but still won his race that afternoon. Three days later he became the shortest priced favourite to win the Melbourne Cup (which was why he'd been targeted).

Phar Lap's owner was an American, who wanted him to compete in what was then racing's richest event, the Agua Caliente in Mexico. Despite the long voyage and a hoof injury, Phar Lap won decisively in record time, cementing his claim to being the greatest horse in the world. This was on 20 March 1932. Sixteen days later he was dead.

The most likely explanation was that he'd eaten grass accidentally contaminated with an insecticide, but rumours of deliberate poisoning spread in Australia, where Phar Lap had become a national hero. Radio programmes were interrupted to announce his death, flags were flown at half mast, and he was mourned across the country and in New Zealand. Phar Lap's skeleton is held by Te Papa, the Museum of New Zealand. His lifelike stuffed hide is on display in the National Museum, Melbourne. And his 7-kilogram heart (twice the normal size) is in Canberra's Institute of Anatomy.

Haru-urara The fondness of the Japanese for the hopeless but plucky underdog turned Japanese mare Haru-urara ('glorious spring') into a national hero. By the time she was retired in 2004 the chestnut mare had contested 106 races without a single win, although she had managed a few placings and earned around $9,000. By then the unprepossessing eight-year-old had become Japan's top equine celebrity. She had rescued an ailing Kochi racecourse by attracting thousands of fans, boosted tourism and the souvenir industry, had a pop song written about her, and was set to star in a movie of her life. Best of all, from her point of view, she had earned a cushy old age retirement, instead of a trip to the slaughterhouse. Which just goes to illustrate one of racing's greatest charms – that while it is all about victory, triumph and glory, sometimes, paradoxically, it is better not to be a winner at all.

Racing vocabulary

allowances (also called 'claims') Apprentice jockeys can claim a weight reduction in many (but not all) races, which encourages trainers to use them more (the lighter weight carried by the horse compensating for the rider's inexperience). Allowances are on a sliding scale: up to five wins, they can claim 4 kilograms; 6 to 30 wins – 3 kilograms; 31 to 60 wins – 2 kilograms; 61 to 100 wins – 1 kilogram.

birdcage The enclosure where the horses walk around before a race, and where they return afterwards. The term is peculiar to New Zealand – everywhere else it's called the saddling or parade ring. It may be connected with the birds that fortune-tellers used for picking out lucky numbers in the old days, but nobody really knows for sure.

black (or **bold**) **type** Used literally in bloodstock catalogues, the bold type shows that a horse has won at a superior level, known as 'stakes' or 'listed' races. Countries compile their own lists of prestige races, which are recognised internationally. At the top are 'group' events. Currently New Zealand holds 23 Group One, 21 Group Two, 34 Group Three and 68 Listed races. Winning such races and being entitled to the 'black type' description greatly enhances a horse's value.

box In greyhound racing, boxes (also called 'traps') are used at the start. These are like little individual kennels joined together – eight in New Zealand, but in some countries there are only six. The wire gates open upwards electronically when the race starts. Inside (1) and outside (8) box draws are an advantage, because the dogs are less likely to be pushed around in the scramble for early positions.

by, from and **out of** When people first get interested in racing, and want to talk about breeding, they often confuse these terms. 'By' is used only for males: you say 'my horse is *by* Zabeel'. Then you say either 'from' or 'out of' when you really want to impress your listener by naming the animal's mother as well. Only novices say 'my horse is out of Zabeel'.

draw/barrier draw The position from which horses start, these days allotted by a computer. Mostly an inside draw (near the running rail) is an advantage, but this also depends on such variables as the length of the race (the longer, the less critical), the way the horse likes to run (some always start slowly, so an outside draw doesn't matter much), the track's shape and ground conditions. The draw is the little number in brackets *after* a horse's name, not in front of it (that's the saddlecloth number). Number 1 is the inside draw.

emergency, or **ballot** Where there are more horses accepted for a race than can start (all tracks have field limits), the remainder are called emergencies or balloted horses, and will come into the field if other runners are withdrawn. They are listed according to their handicap, and re-enter in that order. The same applies to greyhound racing, except there are never more than two emergency dogs.

enquiry In horse racing, enquiries are held when a rider or driver − or sometimes the stipendiary steward − protests against another runner for causing interference. Dividends on the affected runners are not paid out until the protest has been heard. If upheld, placings will be changed − which is why it's important never to throw away your tickets until the 'all-clear' is announced. In greyhound racing enquiries are rare, and never affect the dividends.

entire (Emphasis on the first syllable.) Another word for stallion, or just 'horse', meaning an adult male horse that hasn't been gelded. 'Colt' is the term for entire male horses aged two or three; yearlings are all horses aged between one and two (with their official birthday being 1 August in the Southern Hemisphere, and 1 January in the Northern). 'Filly' is the female equivalent of a colt, after which they become mares. All geldings are called geldings, regardless of age.

fixed odds This is where the dividend is offered in advance, sometimes months ahead of the race being run. You might have odds of 20–1, which means getting a return of $20 for every $1, or 7–2, meaning $3.50 for your dollar (and in addition you get back your original outlay, unlike the tote where it is included in the final dividend). This is how bookmakers operate, in contrast with totalisator betting, where the dividend depends on the total pool of money invested, and the amount bet on each runner at start time. In New Zealand the TAB has been permitted to operate as a bookmaker, as well as running the totalisator, since 1995.

free-for-all A harness racing term, meaning a race open to horses of all classes, without any handicap – sort of the equivalent of galloping's weight-for-age. Intended for the best horses, which can be selected by the club if there are too many entries.

handicap Galloping races are handicapped by weight; harness racing uses distance. (In the old days it was elapsed time.) Theoretically this gives every horse an equal chance of winning, with the best horse carrying the most weight, or starting the furthest back. Official handicappers are employed by the governing bodies and work principally by recent past form, although sometimes other variables, such as age, are considered. The final field is compiled from the topweight down, so in major events many lighter-weighted horses don't get a start.

maidens Horses and dogs that haven't yet won a race. So you have 'maiden races', for animals of either sex. Even more confusingly, horses that are not maidens can start in some maiden races under certain conditions. And two- and three-year-olds having their first start in races for their age group are generally not referred to as 'maidens'. Maiden mares and bitches are those that have not yet been mated.

scratching The usual word for withdrawing a runner from a race before the start. After animals are accepted for races, they can be scratched up to a certain time. After that they become a 'late scratching' – usually on veterinary grounds, but sometimes because they refuse to cooperate at the start. Totalisator punters get their money refunded in such cases, but if you've bet using fixed odds or bookies you don't.

serve (or '**cover**') Terms commonly used for 'mate with' in the breeding world. So a mare is 'served' or 'covered' by the stallion. While artificial insemination is permitted for both standardbreds and greyhounds, only natural service is allowed in thoroughbred breeding. By thus restricting the possible numbers of foals by a single sire, it increases his offspring's value – and his service fee. Top thoroughbred stallions can command six-figure sums per service, and often serve over 100 mares a season, which is where serious money can be made.

sulky The term for carts pulled by trotters and pacers, and surprisingly enough related to the general meaning of the word: sullen and aloof. According to *The Shorter Oxford Dictionary*, a sulky is 'a light two-wheeled carriage or chaise seated for one person – so called because it admits only one person'.

weighing All jockeys are weighed before and after each galloping race, to check they meet the correct weight allotted by the handicapper or the race conditions (such as 'set weights'). Riders plus their saddles, where lead is carried if needed, are weighed together. If they weigh in light by more than half a kilogram after a race, they are disqualified. In greyhound racing, the dogs themselves are weighed before each race, and must be within a certain limit of their registered racing weight, or they are scratched. Only in harness racing is no-one weighed.

weight-for-age A system recognising that horses can carry more weight as they mature, and thus compete on equal terms with others of a different age. Sex also counts: female horses are expected to carry less weight than males. The scale was devised in England in 1850 by Admiral Rous and is still used today, with only slight modifications.

ACKNOWLEDGEMENTS

In addition to information from my esteemed racing col-
leagues (in particular Tony Morris of *The Racing Post*,
England), I have used the following as sources, including
quotations: Ron Bisman, *A Salute to Trotting* (Moa Pub-
lications, 1983); Maurice Cavanough, *The Melbourne
Cup* (Rigby, 1977); John Costello and Pat Finnegan,
Tapestry of Turf (Moa Publications, 1988); Monique and
Hans D. Dossenbach, *The Noble Horse* (Collins, 1983);
H. Edwards Clarke, *Win at Greyhound Racing* (Stanley
Paul, 1974); Sam Fletcher, *Auckland Greyhound Racing
Club – from Drag Hare Paddock to Bramich Hare
Stadium* (unpublished script, 2002); David Grant, *On A
Roll* (Victoria University Press, 1994); Ivor Herbert (ed.),
Horse Racing (Collins, 1980); Garrie Hutchinson (ed.),
They're Racing! (Viking, 1999); John M. Kays, *The Horse*
(Arco Publishing, 1980); William Mackie, *A Noble
Breed* (Wilson & Horton, 1974); Tony Morris and John
Randall, *Horse Racing Records* (Guinness Books, 1988);
Roger Mortimer, Richard Onslow and Peter Willett,
Biographical Encyclopaedia of British Flat Racing
(Macdonald and Jane's, 1978); Mary Mountier and Tony
Morris, *Notable New Zealand Thoroughbreds* (Alister
Taylor, 1980); W.A. Saunders, *Historical Racing Records*
(1949); E.G. Sutherland, *The New Zealand Turf*
(Newmarket Printing House, 1945); Wray Vamplew,
The Turf – A Social and Economic History of Horse

Racing (Allen Lane, 1976); Andrew Ward, *Horse-Racing's Strangest Races* (Robson Books, 2000); Lady Wentworth, *Thoroughbred Racing Stock* (George Allen & Unwin, 1938); Peter Willett, *An Introduction to the Thoroughbred* (Stanley Paul, 1975); Johnny Williams, *Racing For Gold* (Williams Publishers, 1987). Websites: www.greyhound1.homestead.com; www.gulfcoastgrey-hounds.org.

I also want to give special thanks to Luke Radich of TAB Trackside for his invaluable help in checking facts, to Jane Parkin and Sarah Bennett for their editing skills, and to Mary Varnham for keeping me on track.